MW01077395

Hanson-Roberts Tarot Companion

by
Susan Hansson

U.S. GAMES SYSTEMS, INC.
Publishers
Stamford, CT 06902 USA

Library of Congress Cataloging-in-Publication Data

Hansson, Susan
    The Hanson-Roberts Tarot Companion
    by Susan Hansson
         p.   cm.
    Includes bibliographical references
    ISBN 1-57281-128-5 (pbk.)
    1. Tarot   I. Title
BF1879.T2 H337   1998
133.3'2424-ddc21
                                  98-37380
                                  CIP

99 10 9 8 7 6 5 4 3

Printed in Canada

U.S. Games Systems, Inc.
179 Ludlow Street
Stamford, CT 06902 USA
www.usgamesinc.com

This book is
dedicated with love
to my husband Richard
and three precious children
Adam, Richie and Lauren
and to the memories of
my mother Marnie
and grandmothers
Petra and Delia.

*Sincere thanks and appreciation
to Stuart Kaplan and Anne Flounders
for their advice and direction.
Also thanks for advice and editing
help on the manuscript to
Anne Flounders, Richard Hansson,
Janice Doherty, Jeanne Gerulskis
and Irene Tewksbury. Thanks
to Adam Esten and
Cheryl Price for their T.L.C.
of Richie and Lauren.*

Table of Contents

About the Artist

Translucent waters, shining lights, fairy tale illustrations: The Hanson-Roberts deck is a striking Tarot deck that reflects the North Atlantic coastal regions of its creator, Mary Hanson-Roberts.

A descendent of hardy Cape Ann fishermen, Hanson-Roberts grew up amidst the artist's colonies along the rocky North Shore of Massachusetts. She is a full-time artist who specializes in science-fiction and fantasy. The first Tarot deck she remembers seeing is the Aquarian deck by David Palladini. "The beautiful pictures," she recalls, "inspired me to see other decks."

Cognizant of art's role as communicator of an artist's inner vision to the viewer, Hanson-Roberts sees the Tarot as an excellent medium for accessing one's inner vision through the artistic portrayal of ancient symbolism. When commissioned to design a deck based on the Rider-Waite deck for U.S. Games Systems, Inc., she aimed to create a deck with imagery as classic and easy-to-recognize as that in the Rider-Waite. Her own vision permeates the Hanson-Roberts Tarot deck, as on a subconscious level, Hanson-Roberts believes one cannot help but express one's inner self through one's art.

The childlike imagery and fantasy relate to the artwork she creates in her science fiction, fantasy, and nursery rhyme pieces. This aspect of her work may also be a direct influence of the environment she has created in her current Orlando, Florida home: a dwelling so filled with toys and fantasy figures that friends refer to it as "Santa's Workshop"! One also sees in her work the influence of the Victorian artists Arthur Rackham and Edmund Dulac, with their intricately drawn fairy figures and nature scenes.

The cards in the Hanson-Roberts deck are drawn in Prismacolor pencil, chosen by the artist to give her more control over the drawing than afforded by the use of oils. She modestly attributes the luminous effect she brings to her work to "a trick of the medium." But work done with Prismacolor pencil can potentially appear heavy and muddy in the hands of a lesser artist.

Although her body of work includes many exciting projects, such as games, comic books, and a graphic novel based on the nursery rhyme "Here Comes the Candle," creating The Hanson-Roberts Tarot is, to Mary Hanson Roberts, "the most delightful project" she has ever been involved with. She is delighted to share the deck with all who seek understanding through the beautiful Tarot.

The Evolution of the Tarot

Tarot cards have endured throughout the ages and have collected a large following along the way. Containing a fusion of beliefs in pictorial form, the cards have evolved over the centuries through their association with many different religious groups, philosophers, spiritualists, artists, and theosophical societies. Folklore and myths surrounding their use for purposes of fortune telling have added to their mystery and allure.

The cards are divided into two sections, the Major Arcana and the Minor Arcana. The Major Arcana is an allegorical system of spiritual and philosophical wisdom which charts the way to enlightenment. The 22 cards of the Major Arcana are used in meditation and in card readings. They represent major life developments. Believed to be a later addition, the 52 Minor Arcana depict people, places, things, and events.

While the origins of the first Tarot deck are unknown, the imagery of the Major Arcana can be traced back to ancient Egypt. An ancient Egyptian gallery held an initiation path with walls adorned with 22 pictures similar to the Major Arcana. Eleven scenes on each side of the path revealed the rules and principles of wisdom. Initiates were taken through the gallery to study the messages of the paintings. The Major Arcana has been linked to the Cabala, an ancient Jewish mystical belief system. Each of the 22 Major trumps relates to a Hebrew letter. The four suits of the Minor Arcana (rods, cups, swords, and pentacles) are in the Hindu religious drawing of the androgynous Hindu god, Ardhanari. Scholars have also hypothesized they originated in ancient Greece, Fez, Morocco, and China. In 1781, Antoine Court de Gebelin of France wrote the Tarot was actually "The Book of Thoth," a book of secret wisdom saved from the fires in ancient Egyptian temples and named after Thoth, Lord of Magic.

Throughout history, various religions have been banned and people persecuted for their political and spiritual beliefs. To secretly pass on the beliefs, illustrations could be used that would be recognized by the knowledgeable but not understood by others. The 22 Major Arcana of the Tarot do have a religious theme. They illustrate how our earthly souls can evolve to spiritual levels. They include the trials and tribulations one might encounter in a spiritual journey. Perhaps the Tarot represents such an encoding of spiritual beliefs. As the ideas in the Tarot gained popularity, they may have become threatening to rulers who needed the masses to conform to their religious beliefs for reasons of control.

In 1378, playing cards of all types were banned in Germany. Then, in 1450, the Gutenberg bibles were printed in Germany using the first printing press with movable type. The process quickly spread around Europe. Mass communication was now possible. Printed materials of all kinds—including Tarot cards—became more widely available. There is evidence cards were being used by enough people to provoke a Franciscan friar, in 1450-70, to condemn all playing cards including the 22 Major trumps.

In nineteenth-century France, there was a revival of things occult or secret. During the time of the French Revolution, secret societies were sprouting up everywhere. Even Napoleon had a card reader by the name of Mademoiselle Lenormand. (A reproduction of her fortune telling card deck is marketed by U.S. Games Systems, Inc.) In 1856, Eliphas Levi published *Le Dogme et Rituel de la Haute Magie* and was the first to associate the 22 Major Arcana of the Tarot to the Hebrew alphabet and Cabala. These associations can be found in the descriptions of the Major Arcana in this book. One who took interest in Levi's work was Paul Christian (real name: Jean Baptiste Pitois), who worked in the Library of the

Ministry of Public Instruction in Paris. He created a Tarot system which combined Cabalistic astrology with Egyptian symbolism, and related the Tarot to the Egyptian hieroglyphic paintings referred to earlier.

In 1889, *Le Tarot Des Bohemians* was published by Papus (real name: Gerard Encase). He was a member of the Theosophical Society and was involved with the Cabalistic Order of the Rose-Cross. He wrote about the Tarot in association with numerology, The Tree of Life, and the Sacred Tetragrammaon, or sacred name of God (IHVH: Jehovah).

In 1888 England, MacGregor Mathers, pen name for Samuel Liddell Mathers, published a book on the Tarot cards, including their use in fortune telling. He belonged to the Society of Rosicrucians and was one of the founders of The Hermetic Order of the Golden Dawn, whose membership included the poet William Butler Yeats, Arthur Edward Waite, Aleister Crowley, and Dion Fortune (real name: Violet Firth). The Hermetic Order of the Golden Dawn, referred to as the Golden Dawn when used in this book's section of the Major Arcana, was formed in England around the turn of the twentieth century.

Its members combined archetypal symbolism, myth, folklore, eastern and western religions, Christian and Jewish mysticism, history, astrology, alchemy, numerology, and color to design a Tarot deck. It remains the most popular deck to date and the symbolism is clear to interpret, especially for a beginner. Golden Dawn member Arthur Edward Waite designed a "rectified" Tarot deck illustrated by the artist Pamela Colman Smith in 1910 which was published by Rider and Company. Known as the Rider-Waite deck, it serves as the basis and is the inspiration for the Universal Waite Tarot deck by Mary Hanson-Roberts.

Hanson-Roberts is true to the classical imagery, but her own unique illustrative style adds a fairy-tale quality and a sort of magical innocence. These cards seem to be warm and inviting, thoughtful and imaginative; they are a New Age version of the Rider-Waite turn-of-the-century design.

The New Age movement, like the Hermetic Order of the Golden Dawn, exemplifies a willingness to incorporate ideas from many different doctrines. For example, I.M. Pei incorporates the Feng Shui principles of energy flow in architecture. Many in the medical profession combine holistic medicine with traditional. There has been renewed interest in the Tarot as a tool for spiritual development and meditation. It is enlightening that many people who heretofore dismissed the Tarot as only for "fortune telling" now understand that the cards are interesting works of art with a rich historical background and an illuminating spiritual message.

The Structure of the Tarot

The Tarot deck consists of 78 cards. The Major Arcana or "Major Secrets" are cards marked 0-21. They represent stages of spiritual development. The psychoanalyst Carl G. Jung referred to the Major Arcana as symbols relating to the collective unconscious. For example, anyone who looks at Major Arcana Key #6: The Lovers, whether they be a Californian in the twenty-first century or a Tibetan in the thirteenth century, can immediately recognize the reciprocal, pure magnetic attraction and love between the young male and female. This shared recognition is referred to as the *collective unconscious*. It is immediate, instinctual, recognizable thought.

The 56 cards of the Minor Arcana refer to everyday people, things, and events. They correlate to the 52 card playing deck with four additional court cards: page, knight, queen, king. There are four suits, cups, rods, swords and pentacles. Pentacles relate to diamonds, rods to clubs, swords to spades, and cups to hearts. Most Tarot historians believe the 56 Minor Arcana were a later addition to the original 22-card Tarot deck.

Major Arcana

The 22 Major Arcana are divided into three sets of seven plus the Fool.

Keys 1-7

The first set represents the collective traits of the dynamic psyche personified. They are: The Magician, The High Priestess, The Empress, The Emperor, The Hierophant, The Lovers, and The Chariot.

Keys 8-14

The middle set describes the spiritual influence on the soul and how it is influenced by laws of cause and effect. They are: Strength, The Hermit, The Wheel of Fortune, Justice, The Hanged Man, Death, and Temperance.

Keys 15-21

The final set illustrates higher, complex spiritual laws which are at the same time more basic and pure. These cards include: The Devil, The Tower, The Star, The Moon, The Sun, Judgment, and The World.

0 The Fool

The Fool can be placed at the beginning or end, since like the circle, he is the manifestation of pure, infinite energy.

0 Le Fou   0 Il Matto

0 The Fool

0 Der Narr   0 El Loco

A young Nordic boy in medieval garments begins a journey toward enlightenment. The weave on his red shawl is representative of the work before what W. B. Yeats referred to as the "Celtic Twilight"—when belief in spirits and fairies had not yet dwindled. He carries a pure white rose which reflects his childlike innocence and faith. The tiny leather travel bag balanced on a rod holds memories of past life experiences, instincts, and what Jung refers to as the collective unconscious. His fair hair falls in untamed locks under a floppy brown hat. His eyes cast heavenward, and his rosy cheeks, optimistic smile, and swinging gait all reveal his hopeful, live-for-the-moment nature. Purple mountains ascend to the skies on this sunny day of new beginnings, adventures and journeys. The grass is soft spring green and one gets the feeling that although he is about to step off a cliff, a benign spirit will cushion the fall and our Fool will get up, dust himself off, and move on.

In meditation, tuning into the Fool within will call upon the rush of energy and hopeful anticipation necessary for a promising new beginning. In a reading, the Fool inspires us to find within ourselves a positive outlook unhampered by pessimism or fear, and to plunge into a new phase of life, absorbing all there is to learn with a bright outlook and sense of humor.

Divinatory Meaning: New beginnings. A journey. Optimism. Boundless energy. A happy-go-lucky nature. Innocence. Seeing things in a new light. Spirit of adventure. Open-mindedness. Exciting times ahead. Endless possibilities.

Reversed: Foolish decisions. Wrong choice wreaks havoc in one's life. Apathy. Folly. Madness.

I Le Bateleur   I Il Mago
I The Magician
I Der Magier   I El Mago

In a garden bursting with white lilies of pure motivation and red roses of carefully cultivated ideas, the Magician shows us in a bold sweep the source of his inspiration and energy, and how he directs and activates thought into manifestation. The silver divining rod raised toward heaven shines with white light. His wide open shirt shows he has nothing to hide, no tricks or sleight of hand. The Magician has truly mastered the attributes represented by the four suits of the Tarot that lay on the table before him: the cup of water and emotion; the rod of fire and pure ideas; the sword of air and expression; the pentacle of earth and material concerns. He has carefully cultivated his intellect and through sheer will has learned to successfully put ideas into action. His flowing red cape is the color of his vibrant passion and energy. The Magician is a person of positive action, sexually potent with an inventive and active mind. The cosmic leminscate of harmony and eternity glows over his head. The gold band he wears indicates inspired thought. His belt is Ouroboros, the ancient snake who devours its own tail to represent eternity.

Divinatory Meaning: Will. Mastery. Skill. Intelligent, goal-oriented person. Uniqueness. An inventor. A director. Power of persuasion. Active yang principle. Projects with great forces behind them ensure success. Positive action. Talent.

Reversed: Trickery. Fraud. Manipulation of others for selfish gain. Misuse of power. A rogue.

An intelligent and beautiful High Priestess gently holds the scroll of secret knowledge and wisdom upon her lap. She sits between black and white marble pillars which herald the entrance to the veiled temple. Woven into the veiled tapestries are images of fertile palm trees and pomegranates sliced open to reveal their still-intact seeds. The High Priestess is like Sleeping Beauty, the fairy tale princess whose virginity lay untouched, her secret knowledge unrevealed, for 100 years until she was awakened by the prince's kiss. In matters of the spirit, the High Priestess represents the memory, hidden knowledge, wisdom, talents, and intuition in all of us, male or female. These attributes remain dormant until the individual awakens them by searching deep within.

In meditation, one must retreat into passive silence and turn down the volume of our thoughts to allow the intuition to surface as a guide. The High Priestess is at the gateway, before the veil which conceals the secret world of the subconscious, the spirit world of the unknown, and the feminine principles of creativity.

Divinatory Meaning: Wisdom. Hidden talents. Serenity. Mystery. Interest in the unknown. Esoterica. Platonic relationships. Hidden emotions. Virginity. Power of attraction. Beauty.

Reversed: Ignorance. Shallowness. Superficiality. A femme fatale. Hysteria.

A voluptuous Empress relaxes confidently amidst a field of ripened wheat. Pomegranates burst open, pouring forth their seeds. The scepter with which she rules her domain rests easily against her shoulder. Her crown twinkles with fairy lights and represents the love and female productivity of Venus. She wears a heart adorned with the female glyph on her sleeve. Her mystical number three stands for carnal knowledge and offspring. She is no longer in The High Priestess state, but has revealed and expressed herself. She is fruitful and capable of having many children and nurturing them to their fullest potential. The Empress is a warm and loving consort to the Emperor, his comfort and balance. As with the May Queen, things grow, spring, and dance under the Empress's loving care. Like the Queen Bee of the hive who organizes and keeps running the production of sweet honey, she has quite a sting when crossed.

Mother Nature can produce the conditions for daisies to sway gently in rolling pastures or conjure up wild hurricanes and twisters to tear apart the countryside. The Empress is the mother, and as developmental psychologist Erickson wrote, the relationship to the mother is the most important in a child's rudimentary development and determines all through one's life the ability to trust or mistrust, to be optimistic or pessimistic.

Divinatory Meaning: Pregnancy. Plenty. Material well being. A good harvest. Creativity. Fruitfulness. Maternal influence. Explosive growth. Home life. A loving, kind, and sympathetic mother figure. Abundance.

Reversed: Unproductive. Waste. Trouble with pregnancy. Creative blocks. Loss of comfort. Negative influence from a maternal source.

On a throne decorated with the heads of rams, a traditional symbol of the virile male, the Emperor holds an orb of the world he rules and the staff of eternal life. He wears a laurel wreath of victory around his greying hair, the color symbolic of the wisdom accumulated by old age and experience. The mathematician and architect of the modern world, he rules with logic and a patriarchal mind. He is the archetypal father figure, opinionated, action-oriented, and wise. He can be as rigid and unbending as the hard suit of mail he wears beneath the red robe. The cold grey mountains rising up behind him have reached their goal, but without the liveliness of Mother Nature's lush plants and wildlife. This is where the Empress can balance out her Emperor by pointing out the need to allow for the creative, emotional, merciful side of nature. She can be his greatest ally along with the trusted wise council, experts in every field he oversees. The Emperor has learned to weed out the sycophants and deceitful and to foster the conditions conducive to the development of talents of the people with great potential in his kingdom. The result is an Emperor who rules over a productive and orderly world where growth is fostered and developed, and where greatness on all planes is possible.

Divinatory Meaning: Dominion. Worldly power. Patriarchy. A knowledge-able, competent male. A father figure. Male expression. Logic. Reason. Excellent mathematical, technological, and engineering ability. Lawmaker. Government. Executive ability.

Reversed: Ineffective handling of people and situations. Feebleness. Lack of progress. Illogical male. Poor male influence. Chaos.

Two young boys in medieval dress bow with hands in prayer before the Hierophant, who wears the triple crown. He gives the sign of benediction in one hand and holds the triple cross in his other. The triple cross represents the spirit operating on three planes. Three is a mystical number and appears in Christian studies as the Trinity; in psychology, as the mind divided into three parts: the id, the ego, and the superego. His larger-than-life presence is supported in part by the pillars to the church and the podium he is raised on. This is the tarot of orthodox religion, in which the church shows the way to heaven. The keys can unlock the gates to heaven or hell—the pope will guide the two young boys along the correct path. The youth's bowed heads show their reverence for and commitment to the teachings and instructions of their spiritual leader. In medieval times, the church was majestic in size compared to the housing of the day. Its interiors were designed with columns and arches that evoked the feeling of stretching up toward the heavens. Shafts of colored lights from huge stained glass windows would stream over the worshipers, creating an awe-inspiring environment. The church offers a place of faith, comfort, sharing, and guidance.

Divinatory Meaning: Religion. Theology. Orthodoxy. A traditional life. Comfort from tradition. Religious ceremonies such as weddings, baptisms, ordainment, etc. Spiritual development. Conformity.

Reversed: The bohemian lifestyle. A free spirit. A turning away from rigid parameters to explore new ideas and lifestyles. Nonconformist. Rebelliousness.

A neo-Renaissance couple embrace like Romeo and Juliet, in a fresh spring garden, reminiscent of the Garden of Eden. The young maiden has a peaceful countenance as she tenderly embraces her lover. The young man's face, however, shows concern. New troubles arise when making what to most people is the first major independent choice: selecting a mate. The angel overhead offers protection and guidance. She acts as a spiritual messenger who blesses the choice and favors the union. The couple's attraction is a magnetic pull based on physical, intellectual, and spiritual attraction. The woman's long golden hair is strewn with spring flowers Strands of her hair entwined in the lover's hand symbolize the blending of personalities and of finding oneself in the other. The Lovers is a card of choice, of making decisions based on one's own unique preferences, independent of the opinions of family, social strata, friends, and other influences. Meditation on the Lovers awakens the spirit of love to attract and guide us toward a kindred spirit, a compatible mate, the right choice.

Divinatory Meaning: True love. Choices in matters of the heart. A love affair with great promise. Attraction. Reciprocal love and devotion. Harmony and synchronicity between two people.

Reversed: Interference in a love affair. Parental interference. Infidelity. Wrong choice. A love gone wrong.

The Charioteer has traveled under a starry arch, leaving behind the comforts of the city. He has decided the direction he will take in life and is determined to reach his goal. His serious expression portrays his intention to keep on the path. The face of the moon on each shoulder refers to the feminine, reflective side of his nature, which is protected by a tough exterior outfit of mail and metals. Armed and protected, he stays the course in a Chariot drawn by two sphinxes. Their opposite colors symbolize the pulling of the soul in two opposite directions with equal force. The Charioteer needs great strength to maintain balance between the two or else his cart will overturn. He understands this concept which is illustrated in the "nothing is all pure; nothing is all evil" symbol on the front of the Chariot. The Chariot is symbolic of the vehicle one uses to get to a desired destination in life, such as a unique talent cultivated to its highest potential. The Charioteer is the will that drives one to stay on course and to overcome all obstacles. It is a card of controlled drive and great energy which, when harnessed, achieves great things.

Divinatory Meaning: Focus thought and energy on the goal at hand to achieve success. Great control must be exercised to stay on course and attain goals. Obstacles will be overcome. Achievement. Success. Mental strength and excellent focus.

Reversed: Falling off course. Lack of direction. Unharnessed energy spinning out of control. Errors and accidents. A need to focus energy. Inadequate preparation for success in one's life. Speeding recklessly and destructively toward a dead end.

VIII La Force VIII La Forza
VIII Strength
VIII Die Kraft VIII Fuerza

© 1984 U.S. Games Systems, Inc

A woman controls the king of beasts with a gentle touch. Surrounded by the glass mountains that represented impossible feats to attain in the fairy tales of old, she achieves a seemingly impossible goal with little effort. The lion is subdued by intellect rather than physical force. The woman is dressed in neo-Renaissance garments, and a laurel wreath of victory crowns her hair. The cosmic lemniscate above her head symbolizes the harmonious universe, all forces working together infinitely. The woman understands that when forces don't work together, opposition can bring collisions and ruin. The lion represents the dark, unruly primitive animal instincts that would bring ruin if left to run wild. The cultured and refined woman represents civilization taming savage nature, channeling and elevating it to great usefulness. Since fortitude is connected with the Divine Mystery of Union in esoteric studies, A. E. Waite of the Golden Dawn wrote that this card has a sexual connotation: the wild sexuality of the lion is calmed by the gentle touch of the woman, making the lion productive rather than destructive.

Divinatory Meaning: Physical and mental agility. Gentle but firm person. Courage. Ability to channel dynamic, volatile energy into productive uses.

Reversed: Poor mental or physical health. Nervousness. Weakness. Giving in to destructive forces within oneself. Seeing a negative situation and not putting a stop to it.

A wise old Hermit stands on the mountaintop and shines his lantern as a beacon to let others know he is willing to share his knowledge. Inside the lantern burns the six-pointed Star of David. He wears the cloak of hidden knowledge whose hood is the violet color of spiritual enlightenment, clairvoyance, and meditation. He is at a lonely place, even in a crowd, since few others have reached such a high level of intelligence and understanding. He is willing to share this knowledge, to teach those who have a burning desire to understand. The snowcapped mountains allude to his elevated intellect. His long grey beard displays the wisdom of the ages. His walking staff is the rod of pure energy and intellect, one of the four tarot suits. The wise old Hermit abandoned material comforts to live apart from society and meditate. He offers guidance in understanding the forces within and spiritual enlightenment. In meditation, focus on the Hermit for soul searching and self-examination, and to awaken higher intelligence to light the way and illuminate answers.

Divinatory Meaning: Counsel. Wise advice. Introspection. A need to retreat and soul-search. Reflection. An intellectual person. A time for spiritual and mental development. A desire to seek out the meaning to life. Self-imposed exile. Outgrowing friends and situations. A pause to reflect, to realign thoughts, redesign one's life. A search. Pilgrimage.

Reversed: Refusal to listen to good advice. Avoidance of problems does not make them go away. Dry period for a creative person; mental blocks and muddy thinking. Depression. Loneliness. Isolation.

The wheel is spinning forward, building our fortunes steadily up to a peak, then sending us humbly back down. The only certainty is change. The opportunity is present to prosper, in bad cycles as well as good, if one can ride the Wheel of Fortune with grace, in harmony with the workings of fate. Topping the Wheel is the head of the Sphinx, the Egyptian icon that gave riddles which, when solved, would answer complex questions simply. A Divine Plan is referred to within the wheel by the Hebrew letters of the Tetragrammaton and the letters T, A, R, O. There is freedom for the individual to make choices in life, but they are within the confines of one's fate and destiny. Clockwise in the four corners of the card are an angel, a bird, a lion, and a bull. They have been associated with the four mystical creatures in the bible (Ezekiel 1:10, Revelation 4:7), the four elements, the four Christian gospels, and the four letters of the divine name. The wheel illustrates the continual movement of the seasons, ups and downs of life, reproduction, karma, and cyclical motion. The Egyptian jackal, who represents the evolution of lower forms to higher, and the snake, who continually sheds the skins it outgrows, adorn the sides.

Divinatory Meaning: Good luck. An "up" cycle. Good works in the past are enjoyed now. A time when things go well. Good fortune and popularity. A turn for the better. Karma. Make the best of this fortunate time.

Reversed: Bad luck. A "down" cycle. Good fortune and desirability descend. The only way to ride this cycle is to go with the flow and try to work within it. Things will get better eventually.

A crowned and robed woman stands before the pillars that hold the veil to the temple. The geometric cut to her crown is repeated in the diamond patterns of her dress. The four-sided gem in the center of her crown stands for logic, precise measurement of the facts, and reason. She holds the scales of Justice in her left hand and the double-edged sword of truth in her right. The scales are used to balance cause and effect. The double-edged sword considers emotion and reason, mercy and justice. The sword cuts through the veil to reveal the ultimate, pure truth. Her garments resemble those worn in King Arthur's court, a mythical Camelot which has come to stand for a time of fairness, brotherhood, and honor. The cloak she wears symbolizes the hidden workings of spiritual law; its red color refers to the passion of her convictions. Her countenance is firm and her carefully weighed decision is final. She creates law and order out of chaos and confusion. Meditating upon Justice awakens the ability to see clearly and cut through to the true core of issues—the simple truth.

Divinatory Meaning: Fairness in legal matters. A sensible person; merciful yet firm. Correct evaluations and summations of people, places, events. Logic and perspective. Law and order, balance and harmony. Spiritual justice.

Reversed: Unfairness in legal matters. Lopsided decisions. Adversely affected by flaws and loopholes in the legal system. Misuse of justice. Loss in a lawsuit.

XII Le Pendu   XII L'Appiccato
XII The Hanged Man
XII Der Erhängte   XII El Colgado

A man in medieval garments hangs from a wooden crossbar. He has reached a crossroads in his life and is in the midst of making a decision about which way to proceed. He has decided to reject the material ways of the past and desires to find meaning in his existence. To do this, he must enter a state of suspension to allow the direction to come to him from a higher source. His eyes stare straight ahead as if in a trance, and a halo of spiritual illumination surrounds his head. His arms are behind his back and his crossed legs form a triangle. The shape of the triangle symbolizes the ascension of matter, of all things rising to the top. He has descended to the bottom of matter and now seeks ascension. He is in a state of a self-imposed submission, a surrender to the spiritual guide within. Flowering branches represent new and fruitful growth. The silvery pale blue background lends a feeling of fresh air, newness, and open spaces waiting to be filled. The Hanged Man has anticipated this surrender to a higher force and waits patiently.

Divinatory Meaning: Reversal in the direction of one's life. Suspended decisions. A waiting period. Self-sacrifice. A time when it appears on the outside that nothing is happening, yet great internal changes are underway.

Reversed: Stagnation. Growth can only be resumed when one is willing to let go. Mired down by the material physical world. Arrogance.

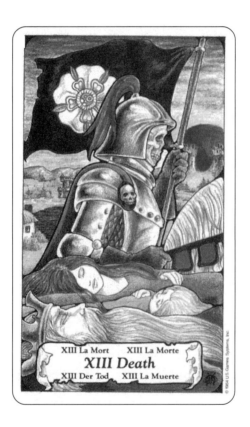

XIII La Mort   XIII La Morte
XIII Death
XIII Der Tod   XIII La Muerte

Death appears as the skeleton of a mounted knight. He carries the banner of the mystic rose, an emblem of new life and hope, as he leads a procession on a white horse in ceremonial bridle. Horse and rider march through the village with no emotion and do not even glance at the king, woman, and child whose lifeless bodies and white pallor reveal that they have fallen into death's slumber. The sun sets between the towers. Life continues on: the tilled fields in the village below anticipate new growth. The Death card reminds that neither important kings nor young children can escape the inevitable end of life. Death destroys the outworn, transforms, and brings renewal. In this card there is a feeling of stillness and quiet; one can almost hear the lonesome flapping of the flag and horse's hoofsteps. Whether it is a death of a person or an event that nature has decided to transform, there is hope. The dead and decaying rosebushes pruned in the autumn will burst forth with new flowers in the spring. Endings can be difficult to endure but they are part of the natural evolution that must occur for regeneration to begin.

Divinatory Meaning: Death of a person, place, or thing that has outworn its time. Fear of death and/or anxiety about endings. Transitions. Transformation for the better. A sudden ending that clears the way for new beginnings. An unendurable situation reaches a conclusion.

Reversed: Stagnation. A situation that has outworn its time lingers on. Changes must occur in order to make way for improvements. Fear prevents one from putting a stop to an unproductive relationship, position, or situation. A close brush with death.

XIV La Tempérance XIV La Temperanza
XIV Temperance
XIV Die Mässigkeit   XIV Templanza

A young angel aglow with spiritual light mixes the effervescent waters of life from cup to cup. Her soft countenance and benign smile show the ease with which she performs the task. Her flowing robe is white, the color of purity. The robe covers a blue garment that symbolizes peace, patience, and serenity. Embroidered in the neck of her gown is a triangle, symbol of the ascension of matter. It is encased in a square, the symbol of logic. Violet, the color of spiritual illumination, appears in the shadow of her glowing, feathered wings. The crown of the spiritual kingdom is seen in the sky above the path between two mountain peaks. Luminescent bubbles of life rise up from the waters. The water on the left represents the subconscious mind; the land symbolizes the conscious mind. The angel balances the two by her position in the middle and the act of pouring the waters. Angels appear as messengers to light our way, heal us, and guide us on our journey. Angels bestow the attributes of harmony, balance, moderation, and control. They teach us to have patience, to realize that all things take time.

Divinatory Meaning: Temperance. Moderation. Balance. The right combination of people and ingredients leads to success. Healings. Working in harmony. Mind, body, and soul working in harmony. Inner guidance. Perfect combinations.

Reversed: The out-of-balance personality is susceptible to alcohol, drugs, emotional or physical dependencies. Not allowing the conditions for proper healing.

The winged green Devil perverts the sign of benediction as he holds reign over the couple chained to his podium. His red eyes burn with an evil glow as he scorches the back of the prisoner who succumbed to his trap. Pointed horns protrude from his head which is covered by matted, unruly hair. The bat-like wings are reminiscent of vampires that fly around at night when the sleeping, unaware mind is vulnerable to the nightmare of the Devil's entrapment.

Throughout the ages in fairy tales and fantasy, evil is personified as a grotesque and ugly creature who can change forms at will to tempt and seduce. He knows only hate and has contempt for the human emotions that he dismisses as weak, such as love and sympathy. He is the ogre, condemned to a tortured existence, who seeks company to share his misery. The lures used are those which appeal to the shallow side of human nature: lust, greed, jealousy, and ignorance. He also symbolizes all things that cause decay and rot, whether it be of the body, mind, or soul. Since these three things are intricately connected, what affects one inevitably affects the others.

Divinatory Meaning: Succumbing to temptation that eventually brings unhappiness. Entrapment. Destructive addictions. Evil. Emotional bondage. Darkness. Superficiality. Obsessions. Confusion. Chaos. Disease which spreads like cancer. Lost soul.

Reversed: Release from bondage. Breaking away from a bad influence. Recovery. Freedom. Escaping from something that would have brought ruin.

Lightning strikes, destroying the mighty Tower and sending its lone inhabitant hurtling to the ground. He doesn't realize that he has been as much a prisoner in his Tower as the fairy tale protagonist Rapunzel was in hers. While Rapunzel was forced to live a life she didn't want and used her wits and hair to escape, this person created his own Tower and didn't even realize he was imprisoned by it. He may even feel deep worry about the catastrophe. Whether trapped in a limiting situation or in one by choice, the powerful forces of nature have decided it is time to dismantle and demolish. Anything that was built on false values won't survive. The occupant must now decide to rebuild the old or start anew.

The dark night sky is filled with turbulence and storm clouds. A full moon casts shadows on the physical and emotional upheaval. A scraggly tree looks as though it has been barren for a long time. A golden crown indicates the lightning strike is actually a flash of insight from a higher kingdom. This insight will help decide what needs to be abandoned or abolished and what if anything, can be salvaged before the rebuilding can begin. Drops of light falling to the ground like scattered seeds mark the beginnings of enlightenment in the wake of catastrophe.

Divinatory Meaning: Problems that have been escalating now explode. An upheaval that breaks apart an existing situation. Divorce. Bankruptcy. Human or natural disaster. Weak foundations crumble. A sudden flash of insight shows that a drastic change, although traumatic, is inevitable.

Reversed: Enduring a bad relationship. Not moving when a move would be beneficial. Letting opportunities pass by. Inhibitions hold one back. Mounting tension and problems have to be dealt with or disaster will strike.

A woman rises from the depths of the purifying water to stare upwards in a state of rapture. Her long flowing hair covers her naked body and she appears to be in paradise. Stars twinkle and shine around a central large star. In a green tree with vines growing up its trunk sits a mourning dove. Red flowers blossom in the greenery by the deep lake. The woman lets the luminescent waters stream through her fingers, and little effervescent bubbles dance through the air. Spiritual illumination has enlightened her, and her face is filled with understanding and enchantment. What was once incomprehensible and difficult to grasp now flows as easily as the natural waves in her hair and water through her fingers. The bold outline around her figure shows her separateness from nature, indicating that individuality still exists amidst comprehension of what the life force is all about. The understanding in her eyes reveals high intelligence. The birds represent the mental activity and the transference of thought from angels to mortals. The bolt of inspiration that shattered the Tower has effectively communicated the enlightening message. The transcendence of thought from above has activated the intellectual activity and provided clarity of thought.

Divinatory Meaning: Inspiration from above. Great ideas. A time of productive intellectual activities. Increased insight. Thought transference. Ideas come easily. Pure expression. Clarity of purpose. Enlightenment. A spiritual calling. Concentrate on the good in life and avoid the negative. Clairvoyance.

Reversed: Lack of vision. Misinterpretations and misunderstandings. Muddled communications. Psychological problems.

XVIII La Lune   XVIII La Luna
XVIII The Moon
XVIII Der Mond   XVIII La Luna

The face of the Moon Goddess is outlined by a crescent in the full moon, the most mysterious, moody icon in nature. It is seen when the world is dark, the work of the day has been finished, and the night hours are left to the imaginations and dreams. In the hours before dawn, the moon watches over our sleep and dredges up thoughts that were hidden deep in the subconscious. They can surface as nightmares or as wildly creative insights. The moon controls the currents which can pull and send emotions reeling and then drown them in the undertow. In an old fairy tale, the moon's reflection in the water tricked the townsfolk into diving into a lake with shovels and pitchforks to try to catch it. What shows on the surface is not always what lies beneath. This card warns one not to confuse illusion with reality. The woman in the crescent of the full moon reflects seriously upon the thoughts of her creative imagination. She sends drops of light to the wolf, dog, and crayfish, who have come out, their instincts lured by the moon's pull. The two medieval towers on either side of the path have an ominous presence, yet instinct and the moon's light compel us to continue our quest and follow the path.

Divinatory Meaning: Mystery. Intrigue. Creative imagination. Unique and wonderful ideas. Psychic ability. Moods. Emotions. Dreams. Reflections. Romantic yearnings. Productive time for artists, musicians, writers, poets, and all creative projects. Soul.

Reversed: Mysteries are solved. Moodiness. Weary mind. Sadness. Anxiety. Frustrated talents. Need for an outlet for creativity.

The Sun shines brightly over a joyous little boy who rides a white horse in a field of sunflowers. The Sun has the blissful, innocent face of a child. Rings of colored light emanate from the center and bathe all with radiance and warmth. The boy exuberantly waves a sun-drenched blue flag. His nakedness shows he has nothing to hide, there are no boundaries to his play land, and he has nothing to fear. The simple joys of childhood are awakened by The Sun. The horse is the one that appeared bridled in the ceremonial procession in Key XIII: Death. Now it prances pure, unharnessed, free from past restraints in a flowering paradise. The four sunflowers stand for the four kingdoms of nature: mineral, vegetable, animal, and human. The stone wall offers protection to let loose and enjoy in an environment of love and trust. All kingdoms are in perfect synchronization here under the protective bath of sunlight. The fresh spring grass has come to life after laying dormant all winter. The perils encountered along the path of the moon have been overcome and now is the time for blissful celebration of newfound freedom, renewal, and rebirth.

Divinatory Meaning: Happiness. Celebrations. Triumphs. Rewards of a life well-lived. Good marriage. Happy family life. Joy of living. Pleasure derived from simple things. Positive outlook. Liberation. Successful completions.

Reversed: Simulated enjoyment. Times that should be enjoyed but are marred by something or someone. Bitter memories of the past hinder enjoyment of the present.

An angel appears from a cloud and awakens the souls of a man, woman, and child. The young family stand in waters where their souls have been purified and they are born again. Trumpets herald the start of a great event. Gabriel blows the trumpet for resurrection; Michael, the archangel of repentance, mercy, and sanctification, alerts the people that it is not too late to heed the call. The benevolent angel awakens the souls of the living and the dead. They bring the opportunity for deliverance and immortality. This the card of the Last Judgment when souls must account for the way they have lived their lives. The sum of past actions and deeds is considered to determine the fate of the reborn.

This is the time to atone for past injustices, make peace, and tie up loose ends. In meditation, Judgment evokes the merciful forgiveness of sins and guides one to the spiritual methods of penance and atonement. With good will and effort, wrongs can be righted and the conscience cleansed.

Divinatory Meaning: A time for answering to one's actions. Spiritual cleansing. Making peace with enemies. Tying up loose ends. Setting the record straight. A time of excellent judgment. A time of being judged by others. Atonement. Rebirth.

Reversed: Guilt. Lying. Fear of consequences for one's actions. Unhappiness. Failure to make peace. Misery in old age.

XXI Le Monde   XXI Il Mondo
XXI The World
XXI Die Welt   XXI El Mundo

A woman with a garland of flowers in her hair dances within a laurel victory wreath. She holds two magic wands and her pure white garment seems to float weightless and free. In the four corners around the card starting clockwise are a bird, a lion, a bull, and the head of a man. These figures have been associated with a vision described in Revelation, as well as representing the four kingdoms of mineral, vegetable, animal, and human. The last card in the Tarot shows the completed work, reward, and the return home. It is the happy ending achieved in fairy tales when darkness has been overcome, wrongs have been righted, and the children find safe refuge beyond their wildest dreams in a magical kingdom. The garland around the ethereal dancer's head symbolizes the connectedness of all things. This theme is repeated in the victory wreath, which also adds a protective enclosure. Paul Foster Case referred to this key as the state of cosmic consciousness, of being one with nature. The balance and harmony strived for has been achieved and synthesized into the whole.

Divinatory Meaning: Victory. Triumph. Great rewards. On top of the world. A new home. Safe refuge. Success that exceeds the expectations. Completion. Excellence. A blending with the cosmic consciousness. Salvation.

Reversed: Earthbound spirit. Mundane attachments. Ruin. Refusal to grow. Stubbornness.

Minor Arcana

Each of the 56 Minor Arcana cards are deciphered by the attributes of their suit, and also by the influence of color, numerology, and symbolism. All 78 Tarot cards are allegorical; that is, each one has a message in pictorial form.

Swords

The sharp, cold, steel sword symbolizes the formative world of expression. Phallic and masculine, swords illustrate aggression, decisions, courage, justice, power, action, forcefulness, alertness, and extroverted thinking. Abstract and clinical, the negative aspect of the sword brings war, hatred, suffering, and destruction. Swords correspond to spades in the modern 52-card deck. The element assigned to swords is air; the season, winter; the astrological correspondents: Gemini, Libra, Aquarius.

Rods

The budding, blossoming rods, colored in warm earth tones of browns, greens, and rose, illustrate the archetypal world of ideas and patterns. They represent the intellect, growth, energy, will, inspiration, and determination. They are strength, positive force, natural action, nature, agriculture, creation, change, growth, and renewal. Rods correspond to clubs in the modern 52-card deck. The element assigned to rods is fire; the season, autumn; the astrological correspondents: Aries, Leo, Sagittarius.

Cups

Cups are drawn as gold chalices. They represent emotions and the subconscious. In spiritual symbolism, like the womb, they hold the essence of the human soul. Love, happiness, human spirit, sensitivity, femininity, and humanity are attributes of this suit. Cups relate to hearts in the modern 52-card deck. The element assigned to cups is water; the season, summer; the astrological correspondents: Pisces, Cancer, Scorpio.

Pentacles

Gold discs or coins with a five-pointed pentagram, is the symbol of spiritual protection (when upright), illustrate the suit of pentacles. This suit represents the physical, material world and its everyday concerns. They relate to commerce, business, the five senses of man, five elements of nature, the kingdom and continuity of life. Pentacles correspond to diamonds in the modern 52-card playing deck. The element assigned to pentacles is the earth; the season, spring; the astrological correspondents: Taurus, Virgo, Capricorn.

Court Cards

The **king** represents the human spirit. He is the personification of the archetypal male with the characteristics of his suit. The **queen** represents the human soul. She is the personification of the archetypal female with the characteristics of her suit. The **knight** represents the ego. Knights represent youth and people, male or female, active in the world and concerned with the development of the soul. The **page** represents the body. The page is the embodiment of immature youth, male or female, still in the developmental or formative stage of life.

Swords

King of Swords

The analytical king holds his sword ready for action. He has learned how to create and maintain order through intelligence and experience. The gleam on his sword infers his talent is a divine gift, and the white dove at his neck indicates he strives for peace. The king started out with passion and aggression, and learned to temper himself and direct his strengths toward achieving his intellectual goals. He has the characteristics of the air signs (Gemini, Libra, and Aquarius). His season is winter.

Divinatory Meaning: A highly analytical, intellectual man who is a leader in his field. Capable and brave, he will defend his ideas or those he favors to the end. He is of original mind; he is skillful at manipulating his environment and people. An authoritative professional type with a big ego that propels him onward. One who comes to quick decisions and is difficult to get around. A no-nonsense type of father, his family may have to learn his methods of reasoning to reach him, as he is not prone to bending rules or accommodating the personalities of others.

Reversed: Strictness. Selfish and uncaring of others. Pleasure derived from ruining enemies. Sadistic streak. Evil. Perverse. Unfair. Dominating, forceful, violent. Preys on the weaknesses in others. War-monger. Bad temperament.

A beautiful, solemn-faced queen stares at the sword she grasps firmly in her right hand. She holds it up in a position of defense, yet her left hand is relaxed and open, a crooked finger seeming to beckon one to approach. Her crown is built into a heavy, protective steel helmet. Her windswept hair, together with the grey skies and turbulent ocean suggest a past amidst action, trouble, and strife. She has the characteristics of the air signs (Gemini, Libra, and Aquarius) and her season, winter.

Divinatory Meaning: An analytical, keen-sighted woman. Her intense privacy is a direct result of suffering in the past. She may be a widow or has lost someone very close to her. She is not a recluse; in fact, she is very sociable without revealing much of herself. Courageous and just, she is an advocate of the fair treatment of others. Assertive and determined, she makes a fine diplomat. Her loneliness has helped her cultivate an inner strength. She is open to relationships, yet unwilling to let her guard down. Very attractive to men who are interested both in a challenge and in a woman who is difficult to get close to.

Reversed: Bitterness and insecurity create an impulse to negate the advances of friendship or love. Fear of commitment prompts her to seek comfort with men already in a relationship. Vicious gossip intended to malign. One who engages in a flurry of activity to suppress deep sadness.

Cavalier des Épées   Cavaliere di Spade

Knight of Swords

Schwerter-Ritter   Caballo de Espadas

A knight charges forward in a windswept fury of unrestrained aggression. One gloved hand confidently wields the sword that took the page two hands to grip. Storming across the countryside, firmly directing his horse, he is experienced, prepared, and competent in battle. The plume in his helmet symbolizes intellectual activity. He wears the fur mantle similar to all the court members of his suit.

Divinatory Meaning: A force to be reckoned with. An intelligent, analytical, assertive person out in the world. A lover who sweeps in out of the blue. Acceleration in all affairs. Things happen quickly in love, work, and social life. Brave and skillful person capable of implementing positive change. Eager to put ideas into action despite all odds. Tendency to be impatient, aggressive, quick-tempered and self-serving.

Reversed: Persistent, aggressive, and annoying. Jealous, possessive, unreasonable, and selfish friend or lover. Beware of trouble or a quick exit. Someone who charges in, creates conflicts, and upsets smooth systems in the name of improvement, and then exits, leaving behind a big mess. Plans go awry.

Valet des Épées   Fante di Spade
Page of Swords
Schwerter-Bube   Sota de Espadas

The page clutches a heavy sword with both hands as though trying to get used to its weight. The serious frown, alert eyes, and hair still swinging from the abrupt turn show a heightened awareness and keen vigilance. He is in the state of developing, as are the budding trees on a plateau behind him. Storm clouds brewing suggest fluctuations of temperament in the youth.

Divinatory Meaning: A youth still getting a handle on how to control and stabilize his/her personality. An assertive individual with innate shrewdness, that, when cultivated, will prove helpful in judging people and situations. Born to be aggressive, this type of person needs structure to channel energy. He/she can eventually be very fair and successful, even if wild or selfish in youth. This person may be attached to a structured program, be it sports, military school, an academy, or trade school. Eager to grow up and get on with life.

Reversed: Wayward youth who involves everybody in the trouble he/she creates. Sneakiness. Voyeuristic tendencies. Spying. Deceitfulness. Mental instability. Feigns friendship, solicits information for future blackmail.

Dix des Épées   Dieci di Spade
Ten of Swords
Zehn-Schwerter   Diez de Espadas

Stabbed by ten heavy swords, a man lies on the cold, grey, cracked, and barren ground. A leafless, craggy tree hangs over him, adding to the horror of the ominous scene. Dark clouds fill the sky and an eerie purple haze hovers over the hills in the distance.

Divinatory Meaning: Defeat and ruin. A tragic end. The lowest point in a cycle. Affliction. Violence. Destruction. The final end to a time of trouble, strife, tension. The cards surrounding this one will indicate whether there has been an actual death or just an ending to a miserable cycle. Although there is a terrible end, it is the lowest point, and things can only improve from here.

Reversed: A crisis passes. New cycle is underway. Meetings with others who have shared bad times or have experienced similar situations prove helpful.

A woman dressed in dark velvet sits up in bed, head in hands, her long hair grey from worry. She is surrounded in the night's darkness, yet she cannot sleep in this troubled state. Nine swords loom oppressively above her. There is no light or comfort; she suffers alone.

Divinatory Meaning: Anxiety. Worries. Insomnia. Solitude. Inconsolable suffering. Bad thoughts that intensify at night or when one is alone. Loss of a loved one. Mental torment. Dread. Unbearable partings. Sadness.

Reversed: Coping by taking one day at a time. Functioning despite fear and anxieties rooted in experiences from which one never fully recovered.

Huit des Épées   Otto di Spade

Eight of Swords

Acht-Schwerter   Ocho de Espadas

Surrounded by eight swords, a tied and blindfolded woman appears to have been captured. The grey waters and bleak sky add to the grim situation. The wind whips her hair around and her expression is one of helplessness. In the distance a castle on the hill has a light in the window as if waiting for her return. The woman's free hand indicates that, with effort, she can escape the entrapment.

Divinatory Meaning: Imprisonment, hospitalization, enforced stays. Desire for freedom, to be extricated from an entanglement that is too heavy a burden. Entrapment. Immobilization. Feeling lost or outside of oneself. The card can also refer to a self-imposed intellectual or emotional imprisonment. A feeling that there is nothing one can do about a bad situation. Isolation. Bad news one can do nothing about.

Reversed: Freedom of movement is regained although difficulties and danger are still around. Release from a bad situation which had seemed hopeless. Escape from oppressive thoughts or situations. Relief.

Sept des Épées

Sette di Spade

Seven of Swords

Sieben-Schwerter

Siete de Espadas

Head down and taking light quick steps, a man sneaks away from camp. He takes as many swords as he can carry. He leaves two swords stabbed in the ground. Tents in the background resemble a temporary medieval camp. Storm clouds are blowing away. Night is turning into day as he hurries away, unseen.

Divinatory Meaning: Theft. Ransacking or stealing. Sneakiness. Behind-the-scenes malice. Warning to be aware of dishonesty in business deals. Lock up and guard possessions. A thief is lurking about. Victimization. Exploitation. Extortion. A confidence is betrayed.

Reversed: Crimes solved. Partial recovery of goods taken. Confessions. Thieves exposed. Petty crimes or vandalism.

A Norseman steers a Viking boat toward peaceful waters and gentle hills. The water churned from his paddle indicates he is in a hurry to reach his destination. His countenance is capable and strong. Silver snakes are entwined around the hilts of the six swords he transports.

Divinatory Meaning: Transport to a calm, safe place after a turbulent time. The move can be mental or physical. Easier times ahead. Problems resolve; trouble subsides. Peace after struggle. A move to a new home. A trip across water.

Reversed: Stagnation. Desire to move to a new place, but unable to act on it. Intolerable situation at home or work. Having to endure hardships.

A bold knight picks up swords left strewn over a battlefield. Two figures huddle in the distance and watch. They are in plain sight, but the knight collecting swords ignores the figures as if they are of no consequence. Purple skies, leafless trees and the defeated pair contrast against the strong but arrogant victor.

Divinatory Meaning: Blatant disregard of others. Spoils of war. Act of aggression. One who makes decisions regardless of what others need or want. Crafty person who works with innuendo and subterfuge to sabotage plans. Trickery. Roguish behavior. Hostile takeover. One who takes advantage of others.

Reversed: Treachery. Loss of reputation. Dishonor. Restructuring after a disaster. Doing what one has to do to survive a ruin.

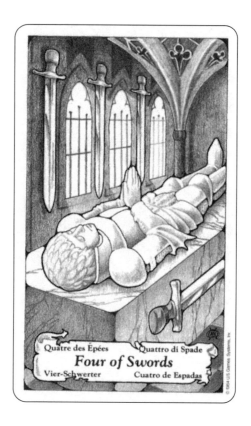

A resting knight lies on top of a tomb, his hands folded as in prayer. His sword lies against the side of the tomb. Three swords hang between three windows. The windows are barred, which indicates the knight is in a place protected from the outside world. The Gothic interior is reminiscent of a church or place of retreat.

Divinatory Meaning: Retreat from the outside world for the purpose of recovery. Convalescence and recuperation. Hospitalization, seclusion, recovery. A need to withdraw and regain strength. A need for mental, physical, or spiritual rejuvenation.

Reversed: Recovery. A healing. Return to the outside world. Return to socializing. Getting back into the swing of things after time away. New relationships.

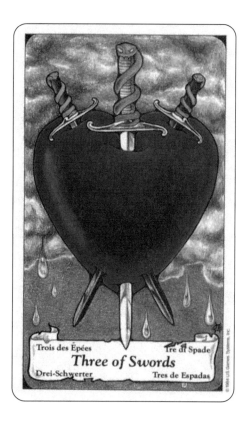

Three swords with evil-looking snakes wound around the hilts pierce the heart of human emotions. Grey storm clouds gather overhead and tears fall from the sky.

Divinatory Meaning: Broken heart. Devastating emotional loss. Separation from loved ones. Tears fall. Intense disappointment. Pain and sorrow. A difficult time emotionally. Helpless to change a situation in which there is intense suffering. Worry, depression, anxiety, sorrow, loneliness.

Reversed: Quarrels and disruptions. Sorrow, but not as intense as when the card is upright. Worry that misunderstandings and arguments may spiral out of control. Regretting harsh words. Disappointment.

Deux des Épées   Due di Spade

Two of Swords

Zwei-Schwerter   Dos de Espadas

A young maiden sits alone on the beach under a crescent moon. Her eyes are covered by a blindfold. She crosses two double-edged swords in front of her. A decision must be made before she can get up and on with her journey. The blindfold indicates that not all of the facts she needs to base her decision on have been revealed. It also denotes a lack of prejudice, of not judging by appearances.

Divinatory Meaning: An important decision has to be made that is filled with tension and anxiety. Pros and cons are weighed but still the answer is not easily found. The decision is being forced when all the facts aren't clear. Stalemate. Truce. Pause in negotiations. Progress is halted until the stalemate is resolved.

Reversed: Decision made, but not without regrets. Movement regained in one's affairs, although something has been left behind, abandoned, or given up. Bitterness and regrets from being pushed to make a bad decision.

A powerful double-edged sword with a jeweled handle is topped by a laurel wreath of victory and leadership. Three rays of white light shine boldly through the grey clouds which have rolled back in the sword's presence. The sword represents justice on a higher plane. The double edge refers to the ability to serve on the physical and spiritual planes, and to see the intellectual as well as emotional side of an issue. Swords represent the formative world of expression. The element for the suit is air; its season is winter; astrological correspondents: Gemini, Libra, Aquarius.

Divinatory Meaning: Boldness and aggression. Great mental and physical strength. Birth of a baby boy. An extrovert. Courage and valor. Strong beliefs. Confidence. Assertiveness. Great force. A powerful new beginning and courage to bring ideas to pass. Brilliance. Excellence in negotiation. Positive action.

Reversed: Failure. Weakness. Poor self-expression. Rebellion. Indecision. Deals that don't go through. Projects that crash. Failure to reach mutually satisfactory terms. Unfairness. Timidity.

Rods

King of Rods

Roi des Bâtons   Re di Bastoni
King of Rods
Stäbe-König   Rey de Bastos

A king, reminiscent of the deep-minded, fair, and intelligent King Arthur of the legendary Camelot, sits in contemplation. A roaring lion, king of beasts, and symbolic of the king's sun sign, Leo, decorates his throne. Steep mountains rise in the autumn skies. His element is fire and the season assigned to the suit is autumn. He has the characteristics of the astrological signs Aries, Leo, and Sagittarius.

Divinatory Meaning: Energetic man with the ability to put ideas into action. Successful and aware of the natural order of things. Comfortable home life, passionate husband, caring father. Intellectual and creative in the business world. Exacting and demanding, he sometimes reveals a fiery temper. Interested in the sciences and agriculture.

Reversed: Arrogant, egotistical, know-it-all. In a leadership position, but not well-respected. Blatantly disloyal, which inadvertently provokes others to be disloyal. Jealous and possessive. Argumentative. Full of ideas that never get off the ground.

Reine des Bâtons Regina di Bastoni
Queen of Rods
Stäbe-Königin Reina de Bastos

The Queen exudes warmth, comfort, and an approachable nature. Her golden hair is entwined with the scarlet ribbons of the rod. She holds the sunflower of regeneration and leans on an armrest of a carved lion. A contented cat snuggles up to her. She wears a pendant of the cross which symbolizes the polarization of opposites. Her canopied throne is decorated with her element, fire. She has the characteristics of the astrological signs Aries, Leo, and Sagittarius, and of her season, autumn.

Divinatory Meaning: Extroverted, she uses gentle yet persistent force to create change and promote growth. Inspires others to evolve upward. Optimistic and intelligent. Able to express ideas in many mediums: speech, writing, art, music. Strength of will to put ideas into action. Loves romance, home life, and growing things. Enjoys children and animals. Prefers a life close to nature. Usually marries, creates a busy home, and is a productive influence in community. Lover of nature, promoter of earth-friendly ideas such as recycling, conservation, wildlife issues.

Reversed: Unfaithful. Jealous and hot-tempered. Overprotective. In a relationship, prone to dominate others but must have complete freedom herself. Weak will. Susceptible to affairs. A fair-weather friend. No outlet for self-expression causes depression and withdrawal.

Cavalier des Bâtons   Cavaliere di Bastoni

Knight of Rods

Stäbe-Ritter   Caballo de Bastos

© 1984 U.S. Games Systems, Inc.

A handsome knight rides away into the distance. His gold helmet is adorned with a dragon, symbol of aggression and fiery battles. Perched out of his view, the dragon also suggests there is a distinct aspect of his personality visible to everyone but himself. Amethysts on his helmet symbolize intelligence. His red cape is ornately embroidered with his suit's emblem and he holds a decorated rod over his shoulder.

Divinatory Meaning: Enthusiastic person interested in learning, travel, people, adventures. Eager and in the process of experiencing everything and forming opinions based on these experiences. Open-minded, intelligent, quick-moving, communicative. Rides easily in and out of love relationships. Not ready to settle down. Creative and talented. Departures.

Reversed: A heart-breaker. A lover vanishes. Infidelity. Moving to a new place. Fickleness. One who succumbs easily to temptations.

A young Nordic page holds a budding rod and cups his hand to his mouth to holler his message across the water and pyramid-shaped fjords. He wears a pendant of an innocent-faced, smiling sun. Gold discs adorn his cap.

Divinatory Meaning: Messages of great significance. A cheerful young person with energy, intelligence, and an irrepressible desire for self-expression. Excellent communication. Enlightening messages delivered in an offhand, innocent way. Musically inclined, creative, and spiritually oriented. Natural curiosity. One who bonds easily with people.

Reversed: Bad news. Young person in trouble. Innocent victim. Immaturity. Too self-conscious. Trouble with adapting to new and/or changing situations. Low self-esteem. Inability to express thoughts and feelings causes depression in a young person. Loss of touch with someone who was of great value and concern.

Dix des Batons   Dieci di Bastoni
Ten of Rods
Zehn-Stäbe   Diez de Bastos

An old man, in Celtic vest, crouches under the oppressive weight of ten budding rods. His greying hair and tired face indicate a great deal of time and effort have been devoted to a project which has now become a burden. His face lights up when he sees the open door of the grey stone castle. The end of his difficult journey is near.

Divinatory Meaning: A burden carried in solitude is near completion. Perseverance. Determination to meet demands. Oppression. A feeling that there is no end in sight; that one has the weight of the world on the shoulders. Completion is at hand. Something that seems like a burden can turn out to be a gain.

Reversed: Unbearable situation finally reaches closure. Release of pressure and strain. Retirement. Rest after extreme expenditure of effort and energy. Freedom to start anew.

Expecting more trouble, a warrior guards his eight rods and holds a ninth in a gloved hand. His bandaged head reveals he has been in battle and his posture is one of defense. He wears a frown and stays suspicious and alert. He is in position to protect against any further onslaughts or attacks.

Divinatory Meaning: Protection of self and others. Capable and experienced handling of challenges and trials. Maintaining one's ground amidst attacks and competition. Defense of one's position both out in the world and on the home front. Good health. Quickness of mind. Protection of what one has obtained through hard work and great effort. Suspicion.

Reversed: Inadequate defense. Loss of interest in maintaining the struggle for attainment. Retreat from pressures inevitably brings losses. Defenses down. Fatigue.

Huit des Bâtons   Otto di Bastoni
Eight of Rods
Acht-Stäbe   Ocho de Bastos

© 1984 U.S. Games Systems, Inc.

Eight rods wrapped in scarlet ribbons fly diagonally from left to right. They are about to land after a smooth, quick flight. Clear skies and peaceful terrain indicate nothing has impeded their progress or arrival. The flight through air indicates intellect, travel, and speed.

Divinatory Meaning: Unobstructed transferal of thought. Messages, letters, faxes. Urgent news. Quick and safe travel by air, land, or sea. Flight. News that travels fast. Vacations, trips of a pleasant nature. Clear expression, communication. Chance encounters of great significance. Arrows of love. Surprises of a pleasant nature.

Reversed: Quarrels and disagreements due to miscommunication. Vacations postponed. Business trips canceled. Important objects lost in transit. Ideas grounded. Breakdown in communication or devices of communication. Misinformation. Misunderstandings.

Sept des Bâtons   Sette di Bastoni
Seven of Rods
Sieben-Stäbe   Siete de Bastos

A Nordic princeling's aggressive stance and look of fierce determination show he is capable of fending off adversaries to keep problems at bay. He is already on a high mountain; however, higher peaks in the distance indicate he has further to climb. There is no one around to help him at this level. This feat must be accomplished alone.

Divinatory Meaning: A capable person adept at staying on top of what seem to be unrelenting problems. Diligent effort and constant awareness necessary to keep ahead of the competition. Defending one's turf. Great effort extended to maintain upper hand. Position of power is being attacked. Fending off a hostile takeover attempt. Maintaining control.

Reversed: Loss of position. Ineffective person. Unsurmountable problems. Defeat. Failure to adequately protect or defend interests. Result of failure has domino effect, causing losses in many areas. Timidity cripples any hope of advancement.

Six des Bâtons

Sei di Bastoni

Six of Rods

Sechs-Stäbe

Seis de Bastos

© 1994 U.S. Games Systems, Inc.

A proud and noble knight returns triumphant. The laurel wreath of victory decorates the rod he holds forth. Laurel leaves also surround his helmet. The horse's ornate reigns and the knight's red cape suggest a ride in a victory parade. His page travels on foot beside him and helps carry the rods. The bright sun in the background symbolizes power and energy fully utilized.

Divinatory Meaning: Victory. Gain. Success. The accomplishment of a great feat. A wonderful performance. Talent, energy, and leadership. The venture or goal will be successful. Great news. Intellect and diplomacy, instead of force, triumph over opposition. Brilliant tactics. Victory after a struggle. Cooperation and loyalty from subordinates.

Reversed: Weak plans. Delays hinder advancement. Lack of success. Apprehension. Fear of enemies, competitors. Pyrrhic victory. Humiliating losses.

Cinq des Bâtons   Cinque di Bastoni

Five of Rods

Fünf-Stäbe   Cinco de Bastos

© 1984 U.S Games Systems, Inc.

Five medieval youths battle vigorously, their rods flailing in anger and aggression. The red-capped individual seems to be holding his own amidst all the competition and struggle. The rods are all in the same stage of development, and the opponents look of equal competence. The battle of wills has escalated into a fight.

Divinatory Meaning: Competition and the struggle for success. Battle of wills. Power struggles. Conflicts and obstacles mar the path to the goal. The fast-paced world requires the individual to constantly improve his skills and acquire new ones. No time to rest. A demanding time of struggle to get ahead. Expect heavy competition.

Reversed: Warning to keep up with the competition. Small problems will escalate if not dealt with. Need to learn new skills. Lectures, conversations. Loss of valued position. Exercise and games. Recreation.

Quatre des Bâtons Quattro di Bastoni
Four of Rods
Vier-Stäbe   Cuatro de Bastos

© 1994 U.S. Games Systems, Inc.

Two Renaissance maidens in flowing robes decorate a floral wreath strewn across four budding rods. They celebrate having attained their castle by the river. The skies bestow a soft golden glow over the scene of peace and glad tidings.

Divinatory Meaning: Prosperity. Well-deserved success. Happy home. Weddings and celebrations. Acquisitions of real estate. Established home and family life. Peace and contentment. Enjoyment of the fruits of labor. New home. Refinement, society, and culture. Harvest.

Reversed: Celebrating small victories in the hopes of more in the future. Some progress, but not as much success as when the card is upright. Moderate success.

Trois des Bâtons · Tre di Bastoni
Three of Rods
Drei-Stäbe · Tres de Bastos

A grey-haired man looks out to sea, awaiting the approach of two merchant ships. Two rods are firmly embedded in the ground behind him. He holds the third rod as a staff as he stands on a plateau overlooking the ocean and beach. Rays of light beam forth from the clouds toward the ships.

Divinatory Meaning: The arrival of help to get ideas off the ground. The use of natural talents to reap great rewards. Partnerships, trade, barter, and commerce. Business travel. Productive meetings.

Reversed: Help offered is beneficial to the one making the offer. Exploitation and usury. Theft of plans, ideas, and creations. Rejected applications, offers, and plans.

Deux des Bâtons   Due di Bastoni
Two of Rods
Zwei-Stäbe   Dos de Bastos

A lord looks out from the ramparts of his castle. The fur-trimmed cape and feathered cap are garments worn in pre-Renaissance times, when the sun was dawning on a great explosion of new ideas, growth, and possibilities. He holds an orb of the world that he is ready to contribute to and explore. The red rose symbolizes the cultivation and refinement of his pure abstract ideas which are represented by the white lily.

Divinatory Meaning: Ready to offer the world one's unique talents. An idea is ready to be launched. Secure environment. Higher learning. Education and practical skills cultivate the ideas of a brilliant mind. Increase and upward swing in matters of growth and accumulation of prosperity. Finding one's niche in the world.

Reversed: Too many projects leave little time left to cultivate a favorite idea or hobby. Too much attention to mundane, trivial matters saps the energy needed to achieve bigger and better things.

As des Bâtons   Asso di Bastoni

Ace of Rods

Stäbe-As   As de Bastos

© 1984 US Games Systems, Inc.

The Ace of Rods, decorated with scarlet ribbons, rises up and a beautiful, soft, pink flower bursts open. A bud and blossom on the stem assure nature's progression in the form of change, growth, and renewal. Clouds billow and gather around a castle on a hill and great rays of light from the rising sun fill the sky. Rods represent the archetypal world of ideas. They represent energy and the inspired intellect, creative and determined. Their element is fire their season is autumn, and the astrological correspondents are Aries, Leo, Sagittarius.

Divinatory Meaning: New ideas, growth, and inspiration touch every aspect of life. Creations, inventions, births. The beginning of new projects sparked by original ideas, and thought patterns. Ideas worth pursuing. Ability to learn, absorb ideas, and create new ones. The launching of an idea that holds great promise. New opportunities for self-expression. The opening of new businesses, the beginning of a new career, adventure, or experience. A time of rapid intellectual growth.

Reversed: Businesses fail, ideas wilt due to a lack of conviction or effort to see them through. Stunted growth. Interruptions in plans cause their downfall. Plans put on hold may miss their time. Cancellations. Lack of personal growth. Failure to convey ideas effectively.

Cups

King of Cups

The king by the sea wears a crown of gold starfish. He holds a gold cup with violet trim firmly in one hand and a scepter in the other. Dolphins, creatures who share his high intelligence and superior communication, rise from the sea behind him. One of his galleons can be seen in the background. He has the personality aspects of the water signs of the zodiac: Pisces, Cancer, Scorpio.

Divinatory Meaning: An authoritative, ambitious, creative man with sharp, clear eyes and keen mind. A deep-thinking leader type. Fondness for the arts. Compassionate. Secretive. Plans things independently and moves on his ideas quickly. Sees no reason to explain or share his motives to anyone, which can be frustrating to those close to him. His actions make sense to others later as everything falls into place—his way. Protective of those he loves. Amorous and passionate. Loves the sea, lakes, rivers, and things related to the nautical.

Reversed: Selfish and manipulative. In a position of power but unwilling to help anyone else. Prone to overindulgence. Persuasive. Crafty. Cold.

A queen like Guinevere, beautiful and romantic, sits by the ocean and contemplates a sparkling gold cup. She seems to be examining something inside the cup, perhaps a vision. Her hair is loosely braided and falls gently past her shoulders. The ocean frolics and bubbles around her. She has the attributes of all the water signs (Pisces, Cancer, Scorpio) and is at peace near water. The face of cupid adorns the arm of her throne. Her season is summer.

Divinatory Meaning: A romantic, attractive woman with a creative imagination. Talented and interested in the arts. Intelligent and thoughtful. Love of home and family. At her best around scenic bodies of water. Keen perception and intuition. Loving and kind, but firm. Understanding and compassionate. Very attractive to the opposite sex. Sensual and erotic. Eternally charming.

Reversed: Selfish and vain woman who uses her charm to fool others. A schemer. Childish and unbalanced. Emotional problems. Immoral. More naive than evil.

A knight like Sir Galahad, the most chivalrous of King Arthur's round table, contemplates the cup of his suit as he rides his white steed through a field. The wings on his helmet allude to Mercury, the message bearer. They also signify imagination and creative intelligence. Although dressed in protective armor, he enters the world using intelligence and sociable nature to obtain his goals. The knight can be either male or female.

Divinatory Meaning: Sociable young person out making their way in the world. Good people skills. Friendly. Romantic, witty, and charming. Strength and sensitivity make this person an understanding, compassionate, helpful friend. Emotional and creative intelligence. The bearer of invitations, propositions, and proposals.

Reversed: Slow to action. Promiscuity. Laziness. Fraud. One who escapes by overindulging in food, drink, or drugs. Superficial charm. Not a true friend. A user. Jealous, bitter person. Entertaining, but snide.

Valet des Coupes   Fante di Coppe
Page of Cups
Kelche-Bube   Sota de Copas

A sweet-faced page stares in wide-eyed wonder at a fish emerging from a cup. The fish represents thoughts emerging from the deep subconscious mind. A shimmering, white glistening light takes the form of the cross. The page is extravagantly dressed, with a feather symbolic of deep thought woven into his hair. An open hand reveals his trusting nature. A giant aqua wave erupts from the sea and gently rolls back down.

Divinatory Meaning: A spiritual, emotional, intelligent, highly-creative young person, male or female. One who wears his heart on his sleeve. Open and trusting. Sensitive to surroundings and others. A young person whose personality is taking form and is just starting to express him / herself verbally and by choice of dress, pursuits, and attractions. Strong feminine side. Capable of deep thought. Enjoys expressing self through the arts. Dramatic and emotional.

Reversed: Easily hurt and confused. Emotional immaturity. Spreads stories, fact or fiction. Harmless gossip. Mediocre talents. Susceptible to substance abuse. Prone to tears.

Dix des Coupes   Dieci di Coppe
Ten of Cups
Zehn-Kelche   Diez de Copas

A couple embrace and hail the rainbow of ten cups while their children dance happily behind them. Rainbows signify beauty after a struggle, reward at the end of a storm. The close and loving family have been together through good times and bad, and now experience their happy ending in a castle on the hill.

Divinatory Meaning: A good marriage. Happy families. Contentment in the home. Successful home life. Close-knit family. People who have experienced trials and tribulations now share the joy of a peaceful, successful time. High self-esteem. Weddings. Security in the home.

Reversed: Trouble in the home. Unhappy marriage. Plans concerning the home or family fall through. Family squabbles. Disastrous weddings. Broken engagements. Bitterness. Gossip and betrayals. Uncomfortable family situations.

Neuf des Coupes   Nove di Coppe

Nine of Cups

Neun-Kelche   Nueve de Copas

© 1994 US Games Systems, Inc.

A plump, well-dressed, jovial man stands in front of shelves stacked with nine upright cups which symbolize attainment and abundance. He is like Shakespeare's Falstaff, the *bon vivant* whose philosophy was to eat, drink, and be merry. The peacock feather and gold necklace show his extravagance and flamboyance. His friendly expression reveals a gregarious, generous nature.

Divinatory Meaning: Wishes come true. Goals attained. Self-satisfaction. Accomplishments. A successful, good-natured person. Good fortune. Great health. Goodwill. Secure future. Relaxed manner. Generosity. Confidence. Plenty.

Reversed: Excess. Overindulgence. Addictions. The personality is too easy-going and others take advantage. Weak-willed. Gullible. Lack of self-discipline.

A woman turns her back on eight upright cups and heads off alone into the mountains. Her cloak symbolizes her withdrawal from society and her personal or secret quests. Her hat symbolizes hidden thoughts. The moon depicts the intensity of the emotional pull to search for something higher. Stars of inspiration glisten over a shiny sea.

Divinatory Meaning: Turning away from established life, friends, and family to search for something higher. A spiritual journey. Looking for meaning in life. A physical or emotional abandonment. A strong urge or compulsion to find deeper meaning. A mid-life crisis. Abandoned success.

Reversed: A return home to an old friend, family, or a loved one. Reunion after time apart. A wayward lover returns. Renewed vision after a physical or emotional withdrawal. Discovery that there have been many changes in your absence.

A wizard-like Merlin looks over a wild array of cups brimming with imaginative, fanciful choices. Stars for inspiration, castles for lofty ideas, a rainbow for hope, an octopus from the depths of the sea for subconscious ideas, a mythical dragon for fantasy, a cup overflowing with riches and a crown for glory, and lastly a fairy from the world of magic. Billowing clouds suggest these thoughts are gifts and talents from a higher plane.

Divinatory Meaning: Creative imagination is a blessing to the artist, inventor, scientist. A person with a lively, wonderful imagination. Talents in many areas. So many interests and talents it may be hard to settle upon one thing to cultivate and excel in. Take care not to get lost in daydreams and fantasies.

Reversed: Ability to focus. The ability to recognize one's strong points and cultivate them. Intelligent choice. Determination. Career success. Recognition. A person with talent and drive.

Six des Coupes   Sei di Coppe

Six of Cups

Sechs-Kelche   Seis de Copas

A sister affectionately puts a protective arm around her little brother as they tend flowers in a garden. They are reminiscent of Hansel and Gretel who cared for each other during childhood adversities and created a bond that lasted a lifetime. The brick wall suggests they are now protected and nurtured in a safe place. The thatch-roofed Tudor cottage in the background represents a secure and happy home.

Divinatory Meaning: Childhood pleasures. Simple, good times. Unconditional friendships. Pleasant memories of childhood. Visits, communications with people with connections to childhood. Meeting with a friend from the past. Happy young children. Inspiration and joy from children. Past acquaintances, things, and ideas resurface in the present.

Reversed: Gifts, inheritances, reminders of days gone by. Returning to outworn methods of behavior when overwhelmed. Living in the past. Longing for the simple days of childhood. The past has relevance in the present.

A depressed man mourns the loss of something that was of great emotional comfort, indicated by the three spilled cups. Like Aladdin, he is outside his castle and away from his love. He now must figure out if he wants to get back in and, if so, under what terms. Transfixed by failure, he does not see that all is not lost. There are still two full cups behind him.

Divinatory Meaning: Depression over loss. Regrets over events that led to the breakup of a romance or strong relationship. Disillusionment. Betrayal. Disappointment with a relationship. Lack of consolation. Unsatisfactory marriage. Concentrating on the negative causes one to overlook the positive. A damaged relationship is repairable.

Reversed: A troubled friendship or relationship improves. Return of an old friend or loved one. Feeling better after a period of disillusionment. Reevaluation and effort reap rewards in a personal relationship. Rebound relationship.

A woodsman sits so deep in contemplation, he is oblivious to the hand issuing forth a cup from the clouds. He seems melancholy and indifferent to three cups set up beside him. He sits under a pine tree where he finds solace and a place to reflect in the deep woods.

Divinatory Meaning: Ennui. Ambivalent disregard for what is offered. A feeling that something is missing. Friends and family offer advice but it doesn't really help. Emotional support and pleasure is available but not exactly what one is seeking. Boredom. Loneliness. Solitude. Contemplation. Reevaluation. Tuning inward to reexamine what one wants and needs to be happy.

Reversed: New outlook on old problems. New friends and acquaintances. Stepping back into the social scene after an extended absence. Acting upon the desire to broaden one's horizons. Self-improvement. Putting forth effort cultivating both new and existing ideas and relationships.

The three sister goddesses of Roman and Greek mythology who dispense charm and beauty toast goblets in a flowering garden. They are known as the Three Graces and celebrate harmony, peace, and abundance. Fruit-bearing trees form a protective canopy above them.

Divinatory Meaning: Celebrations. Abundance. Harvest. Creativity. Healings. Success. Liberality. Successful culmination of events. Happiness. A gathering of friends and families. Harmony. Peace. Marriages. Births. Engagements.

Reversed: Excess. Sensual overload. Too much merrymaking creates problems. Promiscuity and its aftermath. Eating, drinking, overindulging in general. Wanton behavior.

A young Renaissance couple bow to each other in mutual love and admiration. Their pledge with cups causes a white light in the form of a cross to appear. This indicates their union is blessed on a spiritual plane. The Caduceus of Hermes rises above them. A lion wears angel wings to note their animal passion is combined with higher love.

Divinatory Meaning: Commitment. Marriage. Mutual love and respect. Legal unions, contracts of a pleasant nature. Engagement. Partnership. Cooperation. Harmony. Unions that are fated, meant to be. Clear communications and understandings.

Reversed: Divorce. Dissolution of partnerships. Disharmony. Lack of cooperation. Breaking up of legal unions. Broken engagements, contracts. Losing a job or business due to troubled relationships. Jealousy interferes with relationships.

A gold chalice, adorned with jewels glistens magically. It is similar to the Holy Grail, a cup that according to medieval legend was used by Jesus in the Last Supper. The Holy Grail became the object of knightly quests and came to symbolize the search for spiritual enlightenment. Four streams of the waters of life spill forth from the heavens. A white dove of peace flies in the golden sky. Pink clouds billow over floating lotus flowers. The element assigned to the cups is water. Their season is summer. The astrological signs are Pisces, Cancer, and Scorpio.

Divinatory Meaning: Love. Joy. Abundance. The fulfillment of a dream. Birth of a baby girl. Healings. Happiness. Sensitivity. Humanitarian nature. True friendships. Spiritual fulfillment. Success. The ability to create a warm and loving home environment. New beginnings in the sphere of the emotions. Love brings renewal and redemption.

Reversed: Empty heart. Disappointment in things of an emotional nature. Unrequited love. Instability. Lovers part.

Pentacles

King of Pentacles

The King of Pentacles, like his astrological correspondents, Capricorn, Taurus, and Virgo, is a man of the earth. His shrewd, intelligent gaze and serious frown show analytical ability and a fertile mind. His opulent dress, ornate crown, and large castle reveal an attraction to the finer things in life and the ability to obtain them. Grapes representing fertility and bounty grow in abundance around him. The bull of Taurus, steadfast and secure, adorns his purple thrown.

Divinatory Meaning: An intelligent man who generates security and stability. Very successful in business and investments. A wise counselor, devoted husband, steadfast and true. Excellent father interested in the welfare and security of his children. Ability to quickly decipher the true nature of people and situations. Recognizes opportunities and skillfully works them to his advantage. Generous and protective of those he loves. Wealth generated from physical things such as real estate, vineyards, merchandise.

Reversed: Manipulative, superficial man, quick to exploit. Jumps on the opportunity to advance himself even if it causes great misfortune to others. Obsessed with business to the point of ignoring the emotional needs of family and friends. Vulgar. Uninterested in exploring fields outside of his immediate interests. Closed-mindedness. Unfaithful, uncaring husband or lover. Thinks of family as possessions. Ostentatious.

The merry queen wears an opulent gold crown atop her dark hair. Her robe has embroidery similar to the page of her suit. The pentacle she holds indicates her success and comfort on the material plane. The rabbit represents her fertile nature, both mentally and physically. Cultivated roses bloom over her throne, and violet flowers and ripe fruit grow around her. Soft purple mountains rise over a meadow in the distance. The queen's personality is consistent with the attributes of the earth signs Capricorn, Taurus, and Virgo, and of her season, spring.

Divinatory Meaning: A woman attracted to culture and the arts. Charitable and refined, she is in a position of material security and is helpful to those who attract her interests. Open-minded yet conservative in her own life. Fond of luxurious surroundings and entertaining. Zealous in the protection and care of her family. Interested in everyone; gregarious and secure. Sensual and physically-oriented. She can spot and encourages people to cultivate their talents. Successful whether she chooses a life in the home or out in the world. Dignified, well-mannered, and at home in any situation.

Reversed: Self-indulgent and lazy. Ostentatious and superficial. Seeks then exploits the weaknesses of others. Ignores good deeds and concentrates on the negative. Failure to find happiness. Materialistic. Suspicious of the motives of others, even the innocent.

Cavalier des Deniers   Cavaliere di Denari

Knight of Pentacles

Münzen-Ritter   Caballo de Oros

A dark-haired knight in a horned and feathered helmet holds a pentacle in his gloved hand. He stands over a plowed field. Fruit ripens around him. His expression is serious, his eyes have a preoccupied look as though he is concentrating on the future while preparing the groundwork in the present. He is hard at work, his eyes on the goal.

Divinatory Meaning: A trained and diligent person out in the world. A productive person who uses scientific, methodical strategies to achieve his/her goals. Analytical and shrewd. Willing to work hard to create a secure foundation. Interested in the good things in life. Physically active and interested in a traditional relationship. A lover who is helpful, steadfast, and true. A solid friend with many interests.

Reversed: A dull, materialistic, and lazy person coasting through life. Mediocre effort. Low energy. Aware of ways to improve energy and productivity, but lacking the self-motivation to implement them. Lets other people do all the work. Jaded and cynical. Selfish.

Valet des Deniers   Fante di Denari

Page of Pentacles

Münzen-Bube   Sota de Oros

The page has a faraway look, as though seriously contemplating the future. The band around the youth's head indicates the divine gift of bright intellect focused on the physical world around him. The embroidery that trims the red vest reveals an appreciation of fine craftsmanship and things produced in the material world.

Divinatory Meaning: An intelligent youth, well-bred and interested in the sciences, mathematics, education, and acquiring the knowledge necessary for success in life. Willing to extend effort in academics. Sociable and physically active. Bright mind. Observant and quick to recognize an opportunity. Developing skills in the process of acquiring knowledge.

Reversed: Selfish, greedy youth not aware of the bad impression he/she makes. Inability to maintain friendships. Unaware of the reciprocal nature of relationships necessary to lead a healthy and productive life. Lack of imagination.

Dix des Deniers   Dieci di Denari
Ten of Pentacles
Zehn-Münzen   Diez de Oros

A patriarch with a face reflective of a lifetime of serious, intelligent decisions now shares his wealth with the extended family. He relaxes and affectionately hugs a grandchild and pats a loyal dog. A content couple gaze fondly at the affection between the old man and child. The wall behind them indicates family protection and leads to their secure castle. Ten pentacles symbolize the completion of a family fortune that can continue to produce for the generations to come.

Divinatory Meaning: Family wealth and security. Inheritance. Good fortune in a will. Income from investments. Estates. Dynasty. Achievements which bring personal satisfaction, build family pride, and create lasting financial success.

Reversed: Public embarrassments from dysfunctional family members. Bad press. Family problems and humiliations. Quarreling between family members over business disagreements, wills, personal differences. Lack of security.

A luxuriously-dressed Renaissance woman playfully addresses an exotic bird perched on her hand. Flowers adorn her long hair, which is decorated with a pearl and ribbons. Nine pentacles are neatly placed in three arches between her garden abundant with grapes and her majestic white castle. Her relaxed face and graceful manner reveal a woman protected and secure from mundane woes.

Divinatory Meaning: Completion of work. Enjoying the benefits and rewards of success. Relaxation in comfort. Attraction to luxury and finery. Tasteful lifestyle. Opportunity to surround oneself in luxury and plenty. Solitary enjoyment of material success. Secure and protected fortune. Enjoyment of the good life.

Reversed: A need for protection. Fortunes threatened. Ill-gained rewards are exposed. Capitalizing on others' weaknesses. Extravagance and excess dissipate fortune. Beware of swindlers.

A diligent craftsperson intently examines and polishes a pentacle. Tools of the trade—a compass, T square and chisel—indicate he is still heavily involved in his creative work. His smile reveals the love of his chosen field, the pride of accomplishment, and a desire to produce his best. The pentacles on the wall represent past accomplishments in the field.

Divinatory Meaning: A successful career underway. Progress in one's chosen field. Pride in work. Consistent effort and attention to detail. Joy in accomplishments. Financial increase. Cultivated talents, experience, and skill. Excellent reputation. Advancements. Commissions.

Reversed: Loss of interest in work. Sloppiness and distractions cause failure in one's chosen field. Lack of desire and effort to produce good work. Outside problems have negative effect at work and drain energy that should be applied to craft.

A weary farmer rests on his shovel as he eyes vines filled with pentacles. The crop has ripened, yet the pentacles have not dropped. A pastoral scene in the background and rows of a carefully-furrowed garden indicate the hard work and effort expended. He rests on his shovel and wonders when the fruits of his labors will bear reward.

Divinatory Meaning: Waiting for the rewards of one's labors. Quality of past work affects outcome. Hard work and careful cultivation to bring projects to fruition. Rest after difficult labor.

Reversed: Anxiety about outstanding loans. Loans rejected. Ventures that fall apart. Income on hold. Frozen assets. Unconventional income and/or loan sources. Abandoned projects. Concern about uncollected rewards.

A well-dressed, robust, good-natured merchant laughs, pleased to be sharing his wealth with those less fortunate. He holds the scales of balance upon which his money is carefully weighed, and pentacles surround him. He has built up a lucrative career or business, has very good accounting ability, and is charitable. He shares his wealth with two peasant children.

Divinatory Meaning: Balanced accounts. Accumulated security. Generous individual with philanthropic associations. Sharing the wealth. Charitable work. Good-natured person with innate gift to generate financial success for self and others. Pleasure from being charitable. Money lender, accountant, financial planner, investment advisor. A mentor.

Reversed: Unbalanced accounts. Ill-gained finances. Hush money. Money used for manipulative purposes. Financial troubles. Carelessness with funds brings loss. Inadequate protection of fortune. Accounting mistakes.

A battered, decrepit couple wander, cold and miserable, outside the warm light of a stone church. Intricate snowflakes gather as the poverty-stricken pair hobble onward. The woman's careworn face and greying hair indicate a life of hardships. The young man has physical problems which include a bandaged head, bent arm, and the need for a crutch. The warm light from the church illuminates five pentacles within a stained glass window.

Divinatory Meaning: Poverty and despair. Empty soul. No place to go for warmth and caring. Feeling outside of oneself, apart from the everybody. Out in the cold. Physical and mental stress inhibits clear thinking. Not sure how to get back on track. Lack of confidence from too many misfortunes and hard times. Spiritual emptiness. Sadness. Anxiety worsens existing problems.

Reversed: Ability to pick oneself up and start again after setback. Secret loves, secret meeting places. Finding a kindred sprit. Turning away from bad times. Shelter from the storm. Slow but steady rehabilitation. Rebuilding. Regaining. Momentum is regained in financial matters.

An old miser sits on his doorstep and clings to a pentacle. His feet are firmly placed upon two more pentacles, and the one above his head shows his thoughts are obsessed by his material possessions. His doorway is just outside the village where he earns his money. He isn't dressed lavishly, yet he wears the crown of a leader who has had many accomplishments.

Divinatory Meaning: Obsessing about finances. A miser. The desire to hold onto money for fear of losing it. Enjoyment from the stability and security that money offers. Concentration on finances sublimates other areas which could use development. Savings and investments accumulate. Acquisitions. Possessiveness. Frugality.

Reversed: Spendthrift. Expenditure exceeds income. Credit debt. Trouble holding on to money. Too many bills. Lack of finances holds one back from pursuits. Investment losses. Stinginess. Savings are being chipped away. Time to establish new income sources. Anxiety about money.

A craftsperson hammers and chisels three pentacles above a stained glass window. He labors inside a medieval church with vaulted ceilings and Gothic arches. A column with an Egyptian design on top indicates he's exhibited talent in his chosen field.

Divinatory Meaning: Skilled labor. Apprenticeship. The early stages of training and refining one's special interest area of work. Originality. Consultation with employers, customers. Employment opportunities. Building a reputation for good work. Designs, plans, blueprints. Building and architectural projects. Skillful execution of plans. Help is received to get good ideas into motion. Commissions.

Reversed: Unskilled labor. Costly mistakes. Sloppy workers. Loss of employment, contracts. Dissatisfaction with career and work choice. Scattered energies. Not devoting enough time to studies or sharpening skills. Lack of progress in chosen field. Refusal to listen to or accept intelligent advice.

Deux des Deniers   Due di Denari
Two of Pentacles
Zwei-Münzen   Dos de Oros

A young man in medieval tunic balances two pentacles as he dances on the beach. Behind him, a ship tries to stay afloat in turbulent seas. The youth's smiling face and closed eyes indicate he is not worried about keeping his ship afloat, even though it is evident he has to do a lot of juggling to maintain it. The cosmic lemniscate of infinity holds the pentacles and seems to be magically helping him keep balance.

Divinatory Meaning: Maintaining harmony despite external turbulence. Juggling finances to stay afloat. Effort and a balancing act keep business/financial affairs going. Ability to weather storms, stay positive, and pay the bills despite numerous expenses and setbacks. Expert handling of a tricky situation. Juggling ideas, people, projects. Natural business ability.

Reversed: Falling out of the loop. Unpaid bills. Business losses. Checks bounce. Unstable effort. Loss of employment, or for a business person, loss of a good employee or customer. False starts. Difficulty collecting money due. Ignoring the warning signs of danger.

The Ace of Pentacles is depicted as a golden circle with an upright five-pointed pentagram within. The gold-tinged clouds which billow up and around the pentacle in a violet and crimson dawn suggest that it is a gift from the heavens. White lilies, symbol of purity, abstract thought, and renewal, blossom below. The circle symbolizes infinity; the pentagram, good luck, material blessing, the ability to think and produce along material lines, the five senses of man, and the five elements of nature. The element assigned to the pentacle suit is earth; the season, spring; and the astrological signs are Capricorn, Taurus, and Virgo.

Divinatory Meaning: Beginning the path to material wealth. God-given talents reap material benefits on earth. Mathematical, scientific ability. Success, sales, profits. Acquisitions. New employment. Lucky breaks. Financial gain. Security. Stability.

Reversed: Losses. Fear of success. Financial starts and stops. Difficult road to financial security. Interference with things of a financial nature: checks, banking, stocks, inheritances. Miserliness. Avarice.

Meditation with the Tarot

Meditation with the Tarot is helpful to awaken the particular area within yourself that you want to explore or develop. The 22 cards of the Major Arcana are used in meditation since they represent the archetypal symbolism of the major forces at work in life. Meditating on a particular Tarot image calls those subtle forces within us into activation. For example, if you have been in a rut, thinking along the same lines for too long and fearful of moving out of the safe but boring mode of existence you've created for yourself, call upon the whirling energy, fearless, adventurous Fool for release, to open your mind to new ideas. Study the picture and activate the boundless energy of the Fool within. Relax, close your eyes and meditate upon awakening the qualities of openness, pure energy and optimism.

The symbols and stories of the Tarot make it a wonderful tool for meditation. Symbols evoke emotional, intellectual, and psychic responses. The images of the Tarot have been around for so long and have been meditated upon by so many over the ages, the collective understanding and interpretations of the images have strengthened. These symbols evoke responses, whether conscious or unconscious. Art communicates ideas and emotions. The Tarot is a visual allegory of the spiritual journey. Meditation allows one to focus and heighten awareness of a particular aspect.

The following is an outline of the basic archetypal forces each of the Major Arcana represents. Choose the archetype you want to awaken, read the description of the key in the section on the Major Arcana, find a quiet spot and tune into the spiritual message of the Tarot.

MAJOR ARCANA	AWAKENS
The Fool	Primal energy, optimism, childlike exuberance, discovery, adventure, new beginnings.
The Magician	Will, wits, mastery, making things happen.
The High Priestess	Feminine, knowledge, perception, attraction.
The Empress	Pregnancy, maternal qualities, creativity, fruitfulness.
The Emperor	Logical, paternal qualities, executive, mathematical.
The Hierophant	Conformity, orthodoxy, religion.
The Lovers	Reciprocal love, affection, cooperation.
The Chariot	Direction, staying the course, control.

MAJOR ARCANA	AWAKENS
Strength	Mental and physical health, control over impulses.
The Hermit	Soul searching, meditation, guidance.
The Wheel of Fortune	Fate, destiny, going with the flow instead of fighting it, karma.
Justice	Fairness, just decisions, understanding all sides.
The Hanged Man	Faith, suspend decisions, letting go.
Death	Endings, transformation, clearing the way for renewal.
Temperance	Temperance, balance and moderation.
The Devil	Facing fears to overcome them, obsessions, negativity.

MAJOR ARCANA	AWAKENS
The Tower	Breaking up misaligned thoughts.
The Star	Intellectual ability, inspiration, hope, wishes.
The Moon	Psychic ability, rhythm, subconscious, imagination, dreams, artistic talents.
The Sun	Happiness, good health, joy of living.
Judgment	Atonement, repentance, rebirth, spiritual cleansing.
The World	Balanced, happy, productive and successful life.

Tarot Card Readings

Getting Started

The traditional way to store the Tarot cards is to wrap them in silk and keep them in a special box. To read cards, sit in a room where there will be no distractions so that concentration will be at its peak. Sit facing north with legs and arms uncrossed. This body language translates to being relaxed and open to thoughts and impressions. Readings are best done one-on-one. Extra people milling about can be distracting and inhibiting.

The person getting their cards read is often called the querent or seeker. The querent refers to a person asking a question; the seeker implies someone looking for enlightenment. The querent shuffles the cards, being sure to concentrate on his or her own thoughts and questions. The cards should be shuffled while the querent concentrates on putting his or her own thoughts and feelings into them and stops when this has been accomplished.

A variety of readings are outlined on the following pages. First, some commonly-asked questions:

What if a card flies out during shuffling?

If a card falls during the shuffling, take note of it and see if it resurfaces in the reading. Even if it doesn't, it is of interest to analyze. If the reason the Tarot cards work is because of Jung's ideas on synchronicity, which to him meant meaningful coincidences combined with the reader's intuition, then a stray card flying out of the deck is significant.

Each card has a variety of meanings. How do I know which one relates?

The meaning to choose from the variety of interpretations relates directly to your intuitive choice, the house the card falls in, and the influences of other cards in the reading. The following is an interpretation of three cards which shows that if one different card is exchanged, it can alter the whole reading.

Past: Eight of Swords
Present: Four of Swords
Future: Five of Rods (reversed)

Four of Swords, which depicts a knight in repose, is in the house of the present. The card's interpretations include the need to withdraw from society, hospitalization, and convalescence. The past shows the Eight of Swords, whose interpretations include enforced stays, imprisonment, hospitalization, emotional or physical imprisonment, entrapment. The immediate future shows the Five of Rods, reversed, which is interpreted as new skills, loss of a valued position, exercise, and games. Together, it would seem the reading shows recovery from a hospital stay and the need for physical therapy coming in the future. Since the card in the present shows a resting knight, the healing is still in process and the return to physical exercise hasn't begun. A loss in one's position (Five of Rods, reversed) was suffered: however, healing is important now and recovery is on the way.

Past: Eight of Cups
Present: Four of Swords
Future: Five of Rods (reversed)

If the Eight of Cups, which stands for an emotional withdrawal, leaving an established relationship, and turning away from established way of life to seek something higher, had been in the past, the reading would have interpreted differently. The knight's repose now would take the slant of isolating oneself from one's emotional past and the Five of Rods, reversed, indicates a lighthearted, game-playing return to socializing. The Eight of Cups would be a turning away from a relationship, recovering, and an easygoing entry into the social life again.

Past: Eight of Swords
Present: Four of Swords
Future: The Star

If the Star was in the position of the near future instead of the Five of Rods, the retreat seen in the Eight of Cups would take on a spiritual meaning. That is, the knight's repose is now a stage of meditation and withdrawal from the outside world. The Eight of Cups shows the person has already abandoned an established way of life, friends, and relationships, and is now at the point of resting and soul-searching. The incoming card, The Star, shows the spiritual quest will be realized. The Star reveals great insight, mental clarity, and hopes realized.

The meaning to choose from the variety of interpretations relates directly to your intuition, the house the card falls in, and the interpretations of the other cards in a reading. In a spread, the cards should be read together to tell a story, as opposed to reading each one individually.

That example involved an interpretation of three cards showing how one different card exchanged can alter the whole mood. One more simple example: if the Ace of Cups falls beside the Empress, it shows great love coming from motherhood and the birth of a baby girl. If the Ace of Cups falls beside the three of Swords, it denotes a broken heart and a sad end to a great love.

What if a tiny detail in the card captures your interest?

If a particular object in a card grabs your attention, such as a flame in the picture of the Queen of Wands, explore the symbolism of the flame. The Tea Room reading is all about a stream of consciousness, the "noting-first-impressions" method.

What are the extra two cards?

There are two extra cards in the Mary Hanson-Roberts deck. One is a title card and the other shows a young girl on a balcony, lifting the veil, "To All Believers." This can be added to the deck if you want, and read like as the blank stone in the Runes. It shows there is no answer at this time, but instead indicates a mystery area ready for exploration.

Can a reading be done on a person who isn't present?

Yes. A court card which best describes the person can be chosen as a signifigator, or just concentrate on the person while shuffling.

What are the differences in the Major and Minor Arcana in a reading?

The 22 cards of the Major Arcana represent phases in the evolution of one's life. In a reading, they should be interpreted as archetypal forces at work. The 56 cards of the Minor Arcana will be about people, places, and things. They are the day-to-day events.

Court cards represent people. Kings are mature men; queens are mature women. Knights can be male or female; they are generally unmarried and out in the world. Pages are male or female and are young people not yet making their way in the world.

Numbered trumps of the swords are action-oriented; rods are ideas; cups are emotions; pentacles are material possessions or money.

What does a high concentration of a particular trump or number mean?

If there is a high concentration of Major Arcana cards in a reading, it represents a time of great internal and spiritual growth.

Many cups in a reading indicate importance of emotional matters: love, marriage, children, relationships.

Many swords reveal trouble, change, aggression, strife.

Many wands represent growth, energy, ideas, enterprise.

Many pentacles indicate financial concerns: money, business, work.

A high concentration of specific trumps or numbers indicates:

4 Aces	New beginnings in all areas
3 Aces	Fortunate omens, good luck, fresh starts
4 Kings	Important news, swift conclusions
3 Kings	News of conflicts
4 Queens	Great news, important social events
3 Queens	Friends with influence, power
4 Knights	Old friends and past acquaintances
3 Knights	Social invitations abound
4 Pages	New plans
3 Pages	Sociable youth
4 Tens	Important responsibilities
3 Tens	Important business position
4 Nines	Near completion
3 Nines	Correspondence
4 Eights	News, merriment
3 Eights	Travels
4 Sevens	Good luck, contracts
3 Seven	Disappointments
4 Sixes	Enjoyment
3 Sixes	Advantages and acquisitions
4 Fives	Order
3 Fives	Conflicts, bad times
4 Fours	Serenity
3 Fours	Industry
4 Threes	Determination
3 Threes	Deception
4 Twos	Conversations
3 Twos	Reorganizations, recommendations

Celtic Cross Spread

The Celtic Cross is a very popular method of reading because it covers most areas in life. Each card is placed in one of ten houses, or areas of concern. The card that falls on a house shows what is going on in that area. The actual layout of the cards was originally designed with the four cards to the right (numbered 7 through 10) placed *below* cards in the houses numbered 1 through 6. One can actually see a cross this way. However, placing the stem of the cross off to the right takes up less room and is easier to read.

Shuffle the cards. With the left hand, divide the shuffled deck into three piles. Choose one pile and lay those cards out in a spread as depicted.

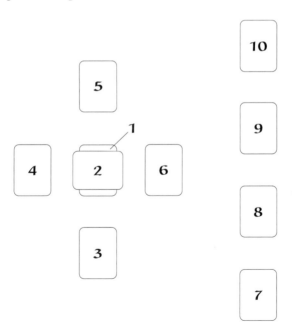

1. *Subject*	**6.** *Within weeks*
2. *Crosses subject*	**7.** *Fears / concerns*
3. *Past events*	**8.** *Family and friends*
4. *Coming in or going out*	**9.** *Subconscious*
5. *Near future*	**10.** *Outcome*

Three Astrological Spreads

The Zodiac Wheel illustration can be used for the following three-card spreads.

I. Zodiac Spread.
Shuffle and divide the cards into 12 piles. Read the first pile as the first house and so on. The houses are charted on the zodiac wheel (page 184).

The twelve houses and what they represent:

Aries	Personality
Taurus	Financial affairs
Gemini	Brothers, sisters, lovers
Cancer	Home life
Leo	Love affairs
Virgo	Work
Libra	Partnerships
Scorpio	Sex, birth, death
Sagittarius	Intellect
Capricorn	Prestige, possessions
Aquarius	Social activities, groups
Pisces	Emotions, psyche, karma

*The zodiac wheel with symbols, signs,
and numbers of each house.*

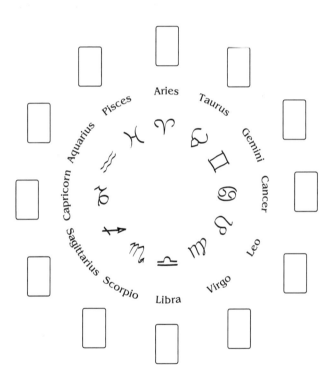

II. Mini Zodiac Spread:

Shuffle the deck and divide into three piles. Choose a pile, and starting with the house of Aries, lay out the first 12 cards. Place them in order around the zodiac.

III. Zodiac Reading for Year Ahead:

Shuffle the cards while concentrating on what to expect month by month in the coming year. When you're finished shuffling, take the first card from the top of the deck and place it on the Zodiac Wheel starting with January.

January	Capricorn
February	Aquarius
March	Pisces
April	Aries
May	Taurus
June	Gemini
July	Cancer
August	Leo
September	Virgo
October	Libra
November	Scorpio
December	Sagittarius

Nine-Card European Method

Shuffle the cards, fan them out from left to right, and pick nine cards. The first three cards are the past, the middle three the present, and the final three the future.

1	2	3
4	5	6
7	8	9

Tea Room Readings

The tea room reading is done as a stream of consciousness. The whole deck is shuffled and each card is read one by one. First impressions should be noted quickly, and then move on to the next card. Do not stop to look up meanings in a book. Try not to break the rhythm or stream of thoughts. This helps develop intuition. Just read what you notice immediately. For example, if you turn over the Nine of Wands and the only thing that attracts your attention is the bandage around the man's head, say so and move on to the next card. This type of reading gives no time sequence and moves quickly, so it is good to jot down or tape record the impressions.

Quick Answers

Shuffle the cards while concentrating on the question. Cut the deck and read the bottom card on the top half.

Closing Thoughts

The Tarot card's beginnings are shrouded in mystery. There are logical hypothesis of its origins, some written about in the first section of this book. The fact that no one knows for sure enhances their magic.

I first heard about the Tarot from my grandmother when I was still in middle school. I had never seen a deck before. However, within a week of hearing about them, a gift shop was just opening in the small town I lived in. I happened to be walking by with a friend and we decided to check it out. The first display I saw was a Tarot deck. It was a French deck and difficult for me to understand. Yet it fascinated me and led to a search for any book or knowledgeable person I could find who could open the door to discovery. Not only did a whole new open-minded way of thinking evolve for me, but an education in history, theology, art, astrology, numerology, and mystiscm. The learning is infinite. I love to hear how other people discovered the Tarot, because sometimes the ways seem just as mysterious, coincidental, or serendipitous as the cards themselves!

The Dedication Card

On a stone balcony, a young gypsy girl pulls back the veil and invites the viewer to explore the unknown, the mysteries of the mind and spirit, through the ancient Tarot.

Bibliography

Benavides, Rudolfo C. *The Prophetic Tarot.*
Mexico: Editores Mexicanos Unidos, S.A. 1974.

Bettelheim, Bruno. *The Uses of Enchantment.* New York:
Vintage Books, A Division of Random House. 1989.

Cavendish, Richard. *The Tarot.* London:
Michael Joseph, Ltd. 1975.

Cirlot, J. E. J. *A Dictionary of Symbols, 2nd Edition.*
New York: Philosophical Library, 1972.

Crowley, Aleister. *The Book of Thoth (Egyptian Tarot).*
New York: Samuel Weiser, Inc., 1969.

Douglas, Alfred. *The Tarot.* New York:
Penguin Books, 1972.

Fortune, Dion. *The Mystical Qabalah.*
New York: Alta Gaia Books, 1979.

Gerulskis-Estes, Susan. *The Book of Tarot.*
Stamford, CT: U.S. Games Systems, 1981.

Gray, Eden. *A Complete Guide to the Tarot.*
New York: Crown Publishers, 1970.

Hansson, Susan. *Reading Tarot Cards.*
Stamford, CT: U.S. Games Systems, 1996.

Hoeller, Stephan A. *The Royal Road: A Manual of Kabalistic Meditations on the Tarot*. Wheaton, IL: Theosophical Pulishing House, 1975.

Jung, Carl G. *Man and His Symbols*. Garden City, NJ: Doubleday, 1964.

Kaplan, Stuart R. *The Encyclopedia of Tarot, Volumes I, II, and III*. New York: U.S. Games Systems, 1978.

Levi, Eliphas. *The Key to the Mysteries*. New York: Samuel Weiser, 1970.

Nichols, Sallie. *Jung and the Tarot*. York Beach, ME: Samuel Weiser, 1980.

Ouseley, S. G. J. *Color Meditations*. Portsmouth, England: Grosvenor Press, 1978.

Papus. *The Tarot of the Bohemians, 3rd Edition*. Translated by A.P. Morton. Los Angeles, CA: Wilshire Book Co., 1972.

Parrinder, Edward Geoffrey. *A Dictionary of Non-Christian Religions*. Philadelphia, PA: The Westminster Press, 1974.

Waite, Arthur Edward. *Pictorial Key to the Tarot*. Stamford, CT: U.S. Games Systems, Inc., 1996.

Notes